Back row: Grover, Bonnie, (babe in arms, Lavonna) Front row: Cleota, Max, Hobert. Rick wasn't born yet.

Sherry and I and our six children
Back row: Mark, Sherry, Hobert.
Front row: Julie, Steve, Susie, Tracy,
and Shelley in front.

Table of Contents

Back row; Mark, Steve.
Front row; Tracy, Shelley, Julie and Susanne.

5

The School Bus
Hobert, Max and Cleota

INTRODUCTION

Sherry and I were visiting Dave and Tracy Pingel in San Antonino, Texas. In a causal conversation I related a time when I experienced deep disappointment almost to the point of becoming depressed in my first assignment after basic training in California. Arriving at F.E. Warren AFB in Cheyenne, Wyoming in the dead of winter, many of the permanent staff were gone on Christmas leave and my first duties were standing guard over the vacant barracks.

The mess hall was staffed with less than experienced kitchen staff, the food looked and tasted accordingly. I was issued a large thick Parka with wool around the hood, much like an Eskimo would wear, which was needed when going from building to building. I began to reconsider my decision to join this branch of the service. These deplorable conditions surely will improve when this base is back to normal operation, I told myself.

Finally, in desperation, I called my dad telling him that I must come home for a while, have someone back there get sick and call the Red Cross and get me an emergency leave. My dad's mother, Grandma Della, was having a minor procedure in the doctor's office; that done the trick. In a couple of days here came an orderly from the first sergeant's office telling me my grandmother was having surgery and I must come home at once. The staff had arranged my travel on a military hop. A plane was leaving right away destined for a base in Tennessee. Once there, I could check for another flight that could possibly get me closer to home. I packed my duffle bag, went out to the flight line and boarded that plane. We made an emergency landing in Denver as one of the engines was on fire. Going to the operations office I boarded another plane destined for St Louis, Missouri traveling with an Air Force General, we landed in St Louis just a couple of hours later; and I hitchhiked home. My emergency leave lasted ten days. January 10th while on emergency leave, I married Sherry McClease and never stayed in a barracks again in the four years I was in the Air Force.

And by the way, Grandma Della came through the operation just fine.

Dave asked, have your grandchildren ever heard this story?" "I don't know, I answered, I have never thought about it," As I considered Dave's question, I was already writing my immediate family about my current understanding of the Kingdom of God.

Taking Dave's advice, I began to send e-mail messages giving excerpts of my life to my children and grandchildren. These emails have accumulated over a period of several years. You are reading my attempted organization of years of writing. I have attempted to organize them into some semblance of order and share them in this book.

Researching childhood memories; made me realize that I have little knowledge of my great grandparents, other than a chance meeting when I was a young child, maybe 4 or 5 years old.

Growing up around both maternal and paternal grandparents I have personal knowledge from encounters with both, some of which I have listed in this book.

As of this writing the year is 2020, I am 84 years old and due to geographical locations, I have several grandchildren growing up without firsthand knowledge of grandma Sherry and me. Therefore, this book is designed to rectify that situation.

As I researched the information; I recalled activities that hadn't crossed my mind in years. The Ridgedale school district always began the school year the first Monday in September. Most students began the school year barefoot, this mode of dress usually continued until the weather turned cold. Wearing shoes in the summer months by the children was only interrupted when attending a special occasion such as a funeral.

A world at war, an enormous depression had ravaged the nation, yet showing the resolution of its citizens our nation moved forward. The rural electric cooperative (REA) replaced the coal oil lights, electric washing machines replaced the iron kettle and wash board. The hot iron that removed wrinkles on clothing was just plugged in and was no longer heated on top of the wood cook stove.

The rural schools, where a single teacher attempted to teach four to eight grade levels of classes in the same room, was replaced with a consolidated school system with teachers that taught a single subject. Our school bus with no windows was replaced with buses that were up to date and every Ridgedale student had a ride to Hollister to school.

I had never heard the term valedictorian, yet that is what I was in the eighth grade at Ridgedale public school. I was chosen to represent the school at the commencement program where I would be making my first public speech. Ridgedale school was closing, we were being consolidated in the Hollister School system.

I was setting on stage with all the board members and the superintendent, I don't remember what I said, but I'm sure mother thought I was the star of the show.

In the row of chairs behind me were girls from Hollister grade school also graduating from the eighth grade to freshmen in high school. Without realizing it I had met the love of my life at age 13. January 10, 1956, five years later Sherry McClease became Mrs. Hobert Youngblood, she passed away in 2017 after 61 years of marriage with daughters at her bedside, leaving a family of 6 children.

This barefoot boy in grade school, now with a top-secret clearance was maintaining equipment that encrypted and decrypted our nations secrets in the headquarters communications center in the pentagon.

And this same boy at age 24 became a Christian. He has established or strengthened churches in his travels in the United States and other countries in the world. His travels have taken him to Mexico, Africa, Europe, Cyprus, Syria, Turkey, Lebanon, Israel and Canada.

My first year of school was not in Ridgedale but McCune, Kansas. During those war years, as a child, I scoured the neighborhood picking up iron items that had been discarded that could be melted down and used for the war effort. The sound of air raid sirens would trigger lights out by everyone, our little town of McCune would become invisible from the air. I often wished for black window shades but instead it was off to bed.

Recalling a household chore for a six-year-old was keeping enough coal in the house for heat. When the weather turned cold, the large potbellied heating stove in the living room was always hungry requiring numerous trips to the coal yard. I would fill the coal bucket only half full so I could carry it without help.

Now I'm trying my hand at being an author, you be the judge. I'm so glad you have joined me on my journey back to yesteryear, so just sit back and enjoy.

CHAPTER 1

A Rough Landing

(Every landing is a controlled crash;
some just do more damage than others.)

The seed of desiring to fly was planted in me years ago, before I was even a teenager. I would watch a small airplane, I assume it was a piper cub, make circles in the Ozarks sky, and thinking, I'll do that someday. Willis a pilot, when on the ground drove a gas delivery truck, bringing gasoline to service stations in the area. We had a gas station but we bought our gasoline from a dealer in Harrison, Arkansas. I never met Mr. Hammond who always seemed in a hurry when driving his truck, he always drove faster than other vehicles on the highway.

The story was told that our local Highway Patrolman once stopped him for speeding and said, "you're flying low!" and asked for his pilot's license. Willis pulled out his wallet and showed him his actual pilot's license. Wayne laughed, told him to slow his truck down, and let him go without a ticket.

The desire of becoming a pilot was present when I joined the Air Force in 1955 and applied for airborne radio operator. I had to be a commissioned officer to enter training as an actual pilot but this assignment would at least put me in an airplane. Passing all aptitudes tests, being approved and on the list to be chosen, the problem was my name: all slots were filled by alphabetical order and Youngblood, Y, was not the first letter chosen. So, I was assigned to the headquarters communications squadron in the Pentagon. Where I began repairing and maintaining machines that encrypted and decrypted messages.

My goal to become a pilot was accomplished in 1972 when I started private lessons in Hannibal in 1969 and completed them in Kirksville in 1972. My test flight was a solo round trip from Kirksville, Missouri to Fairfield, Iowa. I passed and was awarded a license as a private pilot with a rating of single engine land. I now have over 300 hours flying airplanes and several stories which I will share in later articles.

Preflight and Takeoff

Prior to taking off in the type of airplanes I am qualified to fly; there are a series of safety checks that need to be performed. Before leaving the ground a complete walk around the airplane is recommended. Start by checking the engine compartment for oil leaks, windshield for cracks and the propeller for stress cracks or damage. Next, look at the pitot tube for obstructions and sample the fuel in the wing tanks for water. Look at both wings for damage, both leading edge and wing tip lights. Checking ailerons for proper hinge connection. Make sure the elevator and stabilizer on the tail have freedom of movement. Before entering the cockpit check all tires for proper inflation.

Checks inside the cockpit includes all gauges working and gas tank lever set on proper tank. Check all flight controls for proper movement; then when all clear, start the engine. Taxi to takeoff area and facing into the wind with brakes set, rev the engine to 2000 Rpm and switch to each mag seeing a small drop in rpms when on only the right or left mag signifying they are both operational. When clear of all traffic, line up with the runway and start your roll. Remember that speed is your friend. At approximately 80 mph your airplane will want to fly but keep your yoke forward and wait until you have 15-20 more mphs then ease back on the wheel and lift off. Next gently lower the nose and gain more air speed before you start any turn and leave the pattern. Congratulations you are now flying an airplane.

When landing at IRK, the airport in Kirksville, Missouri, my radio transmission would be: *"Kirksville Unicom Cessna 5652 Tango downwind landing runway one-eight (18)."*

   I have just notified anyone, including other aircraft in the area of Kirksville, Missouri, who I was, where I was located, and my intentions of what I was about to do. I was in the Kirkville area, flying a Cessna high wing aircraft now located in the downwind leg of the landing pattern landing to the south on runway 180 degrees.

   A text book landing at IRK in a Cessna 172 required determining the wind speed and direction and choosing a runway that allowed landing into the wind. After announcing your intentions over the Unicom (Kirksville airport radio) adjust your altimeter, which is set at sea level, to account from airport topographical elevation of 981 Ft above sea level. Now my altimeter can express the actual space between my aircraft to ground. Now I am ready to begin the procedure to safely land my airplane. My direction of flight would enter the flight pattern at 800 ft. setting the carburetor heat and reducing the airspeed, a gliding decent begins. With the airplane descending the downwind part of the leg continues well past the end of the runway, making a left 90 degrees on the base leg, then another left 90-degree turn on final turn then line up with the runway for the landing. My goal was to keep the positioning attitude of my airplane level, controlling my descent using the throttle and applying or reducing power in order to touch-down where I had chosen to land. With the flaps down in full configuration, at the last moment, remove all power and flair or stall the aircraft when within a few inches of the runway with no bounce. When on the ground again using the throttle taxi to my final destination on the field.

Emergency Landing

One day when the weather was sunny and in the 80s, I took off from the Kirksville airport with my friends Denver and Donna Cleary, bound for Harrisonville, Missouri. The rental 140 Piper was a four-seater airplane but was usually used for three adults in order to stay inside the weight restrictions. The airplane was half-full of fuel, more than enough to reach my destination. I would refuel at an airport east of Kansas City. We planned to leave Donna to spend time with some friends. The intended private airport in Kansas City was closed and I had to fly on to Harrisonville. This flight was my first time flying into this area and when I was airborne, I couldn't locate the Harrisonville airport.

My fuel gauge was well below my comfort range and I was getting worried. I spotted a gas pump and a small grass runway in a farmer's field. The farmer owned a small plane so I landed there, hoping to buy some fuel. He sold me fifteen gallons which I put in my wing tank. The grass strip was not totally level and I elected to take off downhill. The weather was clear but hot. I got off the ground but the plane just wouldn't climb, I reached two or three hundred feet but couldn't gain more altitude. Up ahead I could see a tall electric "H" fixture, the type that's part of a dam that produces power for a city. I had to make a decision whether to fly under the lines or make a hard left and land in a field. Making the left, required lowering the wing and losing what altitude I had to prevent stalling. I made the hard-left turn and stayed airborne as long as possible to clear the cattle grazing in the field. I touched down and was rolling out when both landing gears dropped in a ditch that hadn't been visible from the air, sheared off leaving the belly of the plane on the ground. The airplane slid on the grass to a gentle stop just short of the fence I was trying to avoid. I opened the door and we all stepped out on the ground safe and

14

sound, a little shaken up but with no injuries. I had tried to miss all the cattle but my prop killed one and my left wing killed another. I called Sherry who came and got us.

The next day, back in Kirksville, I rented another plane and flew solo about an hour. I couldn't let a small accident stop me from doing what I enjoy.

Working as an estate planner representing United Founders Life Insurance of Illinois, I mostly called on rural farmer clients. My sales method was to determine the amount of cash needed if an unexpected death occurred. An actual government final expense form listing assets and liabilities was used to project final expenses. I usually sold a life insurance policy equal to the determined cash needed.

A couple days after the emergency landing, I sold my friend a sizable insurance policy.

I was the top selling agent for the entire company that year, 1974. I received a plaque listing my accomplishments, the traditional sport coat and tie, a large ring with a black onyx setting, and a Benrus gold watch engraved with my name.

My special sales technique was a leading subject addressed by the key note speaker at this end of year sales meeting.

I've had a lot of great experiences, performed successfully in many positions of employment but of all my accomplishments my family is the one of which I am most proud. God gave me a wife of sixty-one years, now a second wife with four more children, nine grandchildren and two great grandchildren added to my six children, making a total of 10 children, thirty grandchildren, and thirty great grandchildren as of 2019. And have a multitude of friends to go along with them, I consider myself rich.

In 1960 I became born again and began serving God with all my heart, the plan and will of God became the defining purpose for my life. To the best of my ability, I've followed Him, I've made some mistakes, messed up, but I'm putting God first in my life, actually hearing what He says. This was one of the best decisions I have ever made. Along the way I've learned that the only thing you have in life that's worth anything is what you've given away. If you've kept it, it's not worth very much.

CHAPTER 2

Times Were Good and Times Were Bad.

My story begins in 1936 in the Ozark Mountains of South Missouri. At that time the Great Depression still raged, nationally, times were not so good. The 1929 economic crash resulted in sky-high unemployment. Americans needing work traveled west to California resulting in the border guard blocking "undesirables," a policy later deemed illegal and stopped.

President Franklin Roosevelt, in order to get people back to work, created CC Camps, (*Civilian Conservation Camps*) some of which were located in the Ozarks. At first, they were tent cities, but were later replaced by wooden barracks. The CC Camps helped young people build self-esteem through work skills and allowed them to send money home. They were active in building the infrastructure of today's national and state park systems.

Hitler's Germany continued to turn a brash shoulder toward the world, the Olympic track star, Jesse Owens, humiliated Hitler's so-called super race, and Italy's Mussolini formed an alliance with Japan, one of a series of events which resulted in World War II.

The Hoover dam, previously called Boulder Dam, began generating electrical power. The average cost of a new house was $3.925.00, the average annual wage in the United States was $1,713.00 annually. A gallon of gasoline cost ten cents, a loaf of bread eight cents, and a pound of hamburger was twelve cents. A new Studebaker car cost $665.00.

17

That year killer tornadoes struck Tupelo, Mississippi. President Roosevelt was re-elected for a second term, Chiang Kai-Shek declared war on Japan, and the Queen Mary made her maiden voyage across the Atlantic. Sunscreen was invented; Eugene Schueller founded L'Oréal, the helicopter made its maiden flight in Germany, piloted by Heinrich Focke. USA Audio Tapes made its first magnetic recording and the Zippo Lighter hit the market.

None of these events and facts made much of a ripple in the Missouri Ozarks. But my birth, July 29, 1936 to Grover and Bonnie Youngblood excited the Youngblood family of Ridgedale, Missouri, a wide spot in the road, located on US highway 65 about a mile and a half north of the Arkansas state line.

In the 1930s, in the Ozark Mountains of Missouri and Arkansas, hospitals were few and transportation was limited so most births occurred at home. Mine was no different. Dr. Cox from Omaha, Arkansas, an old country doctor, attended my birth. I know his wife, who was likely there with him, suggested my middle name, Lemuel. She had a nephew of whom she was very proud with that name. I kept it secret until my teenage years when someone found out at school. To get ahead of the razing and teasing that would surely come from my friends, I told everyone my middle name was Lemuel and acted proud of it. After that no one seemed to care.

I was the first grandchild that lived; a little over a year earlier my parents' first child, a boy, died at birth. He was a breach baby and the doctor, using instruments to turn him, ruptured his spine. I assume that my paternal grandparents, who lived about a mile away were probably there at my birth.

The joy of my birth was short lived, when I contracted double pneumonia and whooping cough shortly after my birth, my family was deeply worried. In the early half of the 20th century, whooping cough was a leading cause of childhood illness and death in the United States, especially in infants less than a year old. Dr. Cox was called again and did all he could, but I continued to grow weaker.

My father went to town to make funeral arrangements for me, thinking I would be dead when he returned. But all the praying people in the area held me up to God and when my father got home, he found me breathing easier and getting stronger.

Pinetop School House, now a Church,
My mother was the pastor

CHAPTER 3

The Old Dutchman Place

When I was born, Mom and Dad lived in a house on the property called "The Old Dutchman Place." Perhaps a foreigner or someone who talked differently than the native Ozarkian had occupied the property that gave it that name.

The house constructed in the 1920's of locally sawed rough oak lumber, gray from the natural weathering of unpainted rough wood, stood on eighty acres. The floors had cracks in spacing between the boards and were uneven. It was built on a foundation of fallen tree logs laid in the form of a rectangle around an indent in the ground. The indented area had been hollowed out by hand to keep the floor off the ground. Floor joists were attached to the logs to support the house. The roof was metal galvanized tin.

My knowledge of that house came from my childhood when it was vacant and I played there. For a season, Uncle Clyde Youngblood, mother's brother, who had a permanent head injury from an oil field accident and couldn't work, lived in the house. I visited him often and, on several occasions, spent the night.

When I was about two years old my father moved our family to a smaller house located on US highway 65. It was twelve by twenty-four divided into two rooms. A wooden platform six feet high, built into the center dividing wall, supported the bricks creating our chimney. Above the ceiling, a metal stove pipe extended through the metal roof to the outside. There were openings on each side of the partition to receive the stove pipe for the cook stove in the kitchen and a heating stove in the living room.

Mother, using tacks, attached felt to cover exposed wood on the inside walls. With homemade paste made of flour and water she attached wallpaper to the felt. Later sheetrock became available but mother, until much later in her life always liked and used wall paper.

The living room was furnished with a bed and a couch. When people came to visit, three could sit on the couch, some on the edge of the bed, others set on chairs brought in from the kitchen. We children usually went outside to play. A heating stove called a King Heater in the living room kept us warm. The little stove would get red hot near the stove pipe and almost dance when dry wood was used for a fire. I would always stay in bed until dad had the fire started.

When summer time arrived and the heating stove could be taken down and stored in the shed, we had lots of room.

Home canned foods, in glass jars, were kept under the bed and mother knew exactly what was there and where it was located.

My first memory in the house came when I must have been a little over two. I didn't know what Christmas was, but I knew the time was special because our house was full of people. A grotesque face appeared in the window and I screamed and hid my face in the shoulder of whoever was holding me. Later, the mask of Santa, and Uncle Clarence Fisher came into the house and I was assured it wasn't real. Nevertheless, I didn't want to touch the mask or even look at it. I never could understand how Santa Claus could get in the house through that little stove pipe, but somehow, he always did.

The kitchen had the cook stove in the center of the room, facing away from the center wall. Mother's cooking space was a cabinet located to the right of the stove against the wall. There was a place for flour and other ingredients and a two-door cabinet that sat on top that held our dishes. Located to the left of the stove was our kitchen table. The stove was far enough from the wall to facilitate the "ole Saturday nite bath" behind the stove. Mother would leave a fire in the stove so we could be reasonably warm. One time I touched the stove with my belly and a blister came up. Mother put some salve on it and it never hurt at all.

Water for our Household

Our water supply was held in a cistern near the back of the house. A bucket hung on the cistern cover for drawing water. I felt big when I could draw a bucket of water all by myself. A bucket of drinking water was always on a table to the left of the door leading outside. A dipper with a curved handle caught the edge of the bucket ready to dip a cool drink of water. The time to get a good drink of water was just after a fresh bucket of water was drawn. I dreaded when people visited who chewed tobacco and used our dipper to take a drink. I always watched how they held the dipper so I could drink out of the opposite side.

Most cisterns were fifteen or twenty feet deep and six to eight feet in diameter. Some water would come in from the surface but most was caught off the roof using eave troughs and down spouts directed through a gravel and charcoal filtering system. We also kept a rain barrel at the opposite corner of the house to catch water. Women liked to wash their hair with that water. It was also used for washing clothes.

At times of sparse rainfall, drought conditions, our cistern would run dry and we would borrow the old two-ton flatbed Ford truck from Uncle Clarence Fisher and haul water from the Rector Springs that was always running water.

On one occasion when I was a teenager that old truck, probably a 40's model with less than perfect brakes, was loaded with a 500-gallon tank filled with water and destined for my grandfather's cistern. A water pipe connected to a water source, every one called it the Rector Spring, could be accessed from the road. The water tank on the truck could be positioned just right and the spring water would flow through the pipe into our tank by gravity. With the water tank full, returning home was the adventure. Grandpa was afraid to drive the truck, so I was the one driving on this narrow country road with a drop-off on the right side. The road was the kind that if you met somebody, one of you had to back up. Grandpa Luther sat there on the passenger side, staring out the window, watching that drop off, giving constant instructions.

"Move over! Move over, he said, gripping the seat with one hand and the window frame with the other. "You're getting too close to the edge, move over! stay to the left! stay to the left!" he said.

You have to know Grandpa; he wanted to tell you how to do everything and I didn't need him to tell me. I could drive that truck.

"Grandpa," I said. "You've got to leave me alone. You're bothering me. Let me drive this truck."

"Watch out," he said, "You're getting too close. Stay to the left. You're getting too close."

"I'm okay," I said. "I can drive this truck."

"You're getting too close, look out."

He kept on until finally, in total desperation, I stopped the truck there in the road, got out and said, "You drive. I can't drive with you doing this. You're going to have to drive."

Now, my grandpa had grown up with horses and wagons. He had an old Chevy pickup that he drove on the paved Highway 65 and occasionally out in the field and up to his barn, but he had never gotten to be a good driver. We both knew he wasn't capable of driving that truck, and probably neither was I, but I was more capable than Grandpa.

"Oh no, no, no you do it," he begged. He promised to cease all instruction if I would go ahead and drive. I did and we took that water on to his cistern. Then we resumed our normal relationship.

Dad also hauled water for home use with a large sled. He would hitch two mules to the sled, tie on several ten-gallon milk cans, and leave for the Williams Spring down in the hollow on our place. He would return with enough water to last for a few days.

There was an Ozarkian story told about this fellow who used raw hide leather for bridles on his mules. He had gone down in the hollow to get a sled load of water and it began to rain. He started home leading his mules. The raw-hide leather got wet and stretched so much that when he got home the mules were still down near the hollow. He hooked those leather reins over a fence post. When the sun came out and the leather began to dry, those mules came up out of the hollow pulling that sled to the house.

Washing was an all day job. It usually came once a month or so. When a sunshiny day would arrive that was warm enough as a wash day, mother would fill a large cast iron kettle with water, usually from the rain barrels at the corner of the house and dad would build a fire under it. Each item of clothing was washed with lye soap on a washboard and placed in the kettle of boiling water with the lye soap mother had made using a wooden washer poking stick to move the clothes around. After a time, the clothes were taken out of the kettle, rinsed in cold clean water, wrung out by hand and hung up to dry.

In winter we wore long handle underwear under our outer clothes. Mother made us wear them until May first, "Else we would get a cold."

We did get to change them on wash day. Believe me, when wash day came, they needed washing. After a time, dad bought her a wringer washer with a crank, that made the clothes dry faster when they were hung on the line.

Hoby and Sherry

CHAPTER 4

Hog killing time

I can't remember a time in my life that my family went hungry. There was always plenty of food. The only items we bought from the grocery store were coffee, flour, meal, sugar and sometimes we ran short of lard and dad would buy a lard stand of lard (this is what we called the container) that mom used to cook for our family. This container was refilled by rendering the fat from hog meat on butchering day. In the spring, when our garden harvest from the fall began to run out, we also bought potatoes in 100-pound sacks and sorghum molasses in a twenty-five-pound lard stand.

Hogs were killed every year when the weather turned cold enough that the meat would not ruin while it was curing. It had to be twenty degrees or so. Usually, the neighbors would come to help. A sixty-gallon barrel of water was heated over an open fire. We usually shot the hog in the head with a 22 rifle and then cut its throat to let it bleed out. Then using a block and tackle tied to a limb of the tree the hog was lowered into the boiling water and removed quickly. The hair could then be scrapped off leaving just the hide of the hog. It was then cut up into different cuts of meat. Bacon and slab meat were cured with salt, hams and shoulders were smoked.

Mother never wasted any part of the hog, the head was boiled, and all meat was removed and made into mincemeat pies. At this time in the year fresh meat was abundant. Fresh eggs, bacon, or pork tenderloin, homemade biscuits, flour gravy, and homemade jelly for breakfast made all the work worthwhile.

One time when I was about nine years old, I watched the guys processing a large hog and my Uncle Clarence, the one with the Santa mask, came over to me. The hog had been scraped and was ready to be cut up.

"Hobert," he said," Your finger is longer than that hog's tail." A hog's tail is curly and this dead hog's tail was no exception. I could tell he was wrong so I argued with him and we made some sort of a bet. He held my hand and I straightened out my finger to measure and show him that he was wrong and he pushed my finger up that hog's rear end. I was so mad I couldn't see straight. Boy, had I been had.

No Super Markets

Most of our laying hens laid their eggs in nest boxes in the chicken house. There were times when a laying hen would hide out her nest. She would build her nest in the tall weeds, cackle when she laid an egg, then I would outsmart the hen. I would go to the sound and often find the nest and take the egg to mother.

Now and then mom permitted a 'setting hen' to lay several eggs in the hidden nest and allow them to hatch. The hen would keep all her chicks with her until they were mature. She would watch over and attack anything or anyone who threatened their safety. We made sure there was adequate food available for them to mature. Young roosters were destined for the frying pan; the young hens became layers.

Occasionally a hen would decide to set (incubate eggs) in a nest in the chicken house. Mom would make sure the hen had 12 to 15 eggs to incubate. These eggs would be marked with pencil marks so when we gathered the eggs, we could remove any unmarked eggs that another hen had laid in the nest.

Sometimes a particular hen would not lay in an empty nest. A nest egg was needed. A porcelain doorknob placed in the nest did the trick, then the hen would use the nest.

To provide chickens for meat, newly-hatched chicks were purchased by the dozen from the hatchery and sent to us thru the mail. The mail carrier couldn't deliver them so we picked them up at the post office. We raised them until they weighed two and a half to three pounds and then we had a chicken killing. The dead chickens were dipped in hot water and the feathers were plucked off by hand. The chickens were cut up and stored in a locker plant in Branson, Missouri. The feathers were all saved, washed and dried; used to make pillows and mattresses.

Electricity wasn't available to rural households. The locker plant in Branson produced ice for both commercial and domestic use. Space could be rented by individuals to store household meat.

The REA (Rural Electric Association) had just began constructing electric lines to serve rural consumers. George Kellett, a local soldier, had lost his life in World War II. His wife and small son, with cerebral palsy, lived in our neighborhood and when the REA officials learned about this family, our area received preference and received electricity before other larger areas.

Until their house was wired for electricity and appliances could be obtained my grandparents bought ice from the iceman who ran a daily route. A large card visible from the road contained four sizes of ice, twenty-five, fifty, seventy-five and a hundred pounds. The card was placed in the window with the amount they wanted on top. The ice man would drive to the house, look at the card, and deliver the amount of ice indicated.

An icebox had two compartments. Fifty pounds of ice was wrapped in burlap and placed in the lower compartment; food was stored in the top one. Generally, the compartment stayed cold enough to keep milk an extra day before spoiling. This system wasn't very effective in the heat of summer but that extra day was important.

Sometimes milk and butter were placed in a bucket and hung in the well or cistern just above the water level where the temperature was in the sixty-degree level. Others used their cellars to gain an extra day or two for preserving food; both methods allowed some extra time before the items spoiled. When the REA turned on the electricity to the Ridgedale area the Frigidaire refrigerator put the ice man out of business and the Branson Locker Plant closed.

Our vegetables were what we grew in the garden and/or harvested wild from the fields. Sheep sorrel, dandelion, turnip, polk, and mustard greens as well as wild onions, in season, in one form or another were always on our table. Polk greens have to be harvested before they grow too large and become pithy. I never acquired a taste for rhubarb or goose berries which were often available. Black walnuts and hickory nuts were used in baking. The Rector Spring continued to provide a source of water even in times of drought and was visited by many who lived out on the ridge. There, I was allowed to hold a salamander that thrived in the clear water. In season, a trip to the spring yielded a supply of water cress and fruit from the pawpaw and persimmon trees.

A castrated bull calf, previously designated a butcher beef, would be corn fed until it reached a weight of 300 or 400 pounds and then butchered.

Wild game was also a meat source. We harvested an occasional deer and hunted squirrel often. A good squirrel dog was important as it made the extra meat possible needed to supplement our diet. Squirrel and/or rabbit and dumplings are hard to beat.

Fried squirrel and rabbit for breakfast was a meal we all looked forward to. A rabbit trap (also called a "rabbit gum") is a box twenty-four inches long and constructed of two-by-four by ten-inch boards. A trap door would close when the rabbit entered to eat the apple core attached to the home-made trigger. The two-inch lumber was necessary because the rabbit would chew out if you used one-inch boards. An effective bait we sometimes used was a short corn cob with some corn still attached.

During the winter hardly a week went by that we didn't catch several rabbits. Early in the morning Max and I, and occasionally Cleota, would run the traps. It was such excitement to see the trap sprung and know we could bring home fresh meat. Mom would praise us for a job well done as we ate our breakfast of wild rabbit, gravy, biscuits, and eggs. Wild rabbits are susceptible to a variety of diseases; the sickly ones die when the weather turns really cold. After the first hard freeze it is safe to eat them.

Mark

The grand children at Christmas time
at grandpa and grandma's house

CHAPTER 5

Life Without Electricity

My childhood of no electricity, indoor-plumbing, radio, television, or telephone was filled with mostly outdoor activities. Missing those amenities that we now take for granted was an adventure rather than a hindrance. We did have a battery radio. On Saturday night my father would remove the battery from the car, bring it into the house and we would listen to the world news and the Grand Ole Opry. One of the women singers, Texas Ruby, had a deep voice and sounded like a man.

Our day lasted as long as there was daylight. When darkness fell, we used coal oil or kerosene lamps (kerosene and coal oil are both colorless and thin, and provide identical uses; coal oil is manufactured from oily coal and kerosene is a by-product of crude oil). The glass globes of the lamps needed washing regularly to keep the light bright. Trimming the wicks also brightened the light.

We also used coal oil or kerosene to start a fire in a brush pile when land was cleared for farming. Most children went barefoot from May until October and wore no shoes the first month of school. Walking on the flint rocks without any pain was easy as our feet became toughened. But occasionally, we would step on a nail protruding up from a board. In that case, our foot was submerged in kerosene/coal oil to prevent infection. A gallon, as I recall, cost fifteen cents.

When I spent the night with dad's parents, Grandpa Luther and Grandma Della; we would sit out on the porch after dark, listening to

33

the frogs in the pond at the front of the house, trying to determine what the frogs were saying.

Since I was the first grandchild on my dad's side, my early years were celebrated by my parents and my father's parents, aunts, and uncles. My paternal aunts were Lora Dean and Lodema (Chattie), and Ernestine who died at an early age. My uncles were Cleo, Delton (Buck), and Bueford. The family couldn't go to bed without coming out and checking on how I was doing. The relationship with my family stayed strong until their deaths.

My birthdays were celebrated with big dinners attended by the whole family. When asked what I wanted for my birthday my reply was always "chicken and britches." And that is what I received, a large chicken, pan-fried with biscuits and gravy and a new pair of overalls. Until this day, my favorite food is fried chicken, and of course biscuits and gravy.

My young life was spent in the Ridgedale area (except for the years in McCune, Kansas). An occasional twenty-three-mile trip south to Harrison, Arkansas for groceries and farm equipment and a ten-mile trip north to Branson, Missouri to the locker plant was the extent of my travels.

Winter Time Income.

Usually, we milked by hand eight to ten cows' night and morning. We tried to get the milking done early since it got dark early and there were no electric lights in the barn. In case of an emergency the kerosene lantern hanging by a hook on the post in the barn was used. Rubber boots were a requirement if it had rained and the barn lot was muddy. With a six-quart milk bucket between your legs as you sat on a one-legged stool using both hands and tried to make as much foam as possible as you milked your cow. Foam on your bucket was an indication of speed and the force your stream of milk entered your bucket. Cats were always around the barn and I could hit the cats between the eyes at ten to twelve feet with a stream of milk. Usually, a container was available to feed the cats that hung around the barn

34

at milking time. A ten-gallon milk can was available for you to empty the full milk buckets into. Sometimes a cow would have a sore teat and would kick forward hitting your bucket spilling the milk. I always put kickers on my cows that prevented them from reaching my bucket if they kicked forward.

The milk had many uses. Mother would keep a container in the refrigerator for cooking and family milk to drink. She would skim off the cream and churn butter. I often used some of the cream for my blackberry and huckleberry cobbler, and breakfast cereal such as rice and oat meal.

Much of the milk was put through a milk separator taking out the cream. The cream was put into a special cream can and sent by the rural mail carrier to the creamery in Branson. Soon a check would come in the mail from the creamery in payment for our cream. Soon another full cream can would be on the way to the creamery. This was money for our household needs that we couldn't provide by canning or growing etc. After the cream was removed from the whole milk that left a product I call "blue john." This is what we used for hog feed. B.J. was mixed with household waste water (dish water and other waste products were kept in the "slop bucket") with a product we called shorts and poured into a trough used to slop our hogs. I think shorts was grain produced and pulverized very fine with a consistency much like flour. I just can't buy 2% percent milk; it reminds me of 1% blue john.

The sounds of my childhood that linger in my memory are the clop, clop, clopping sound made by the hoofs of the mules striking the paved highway as I rode home with my grandpa in his rubber tire wagon. Waking up to the sound of crows, the distant cows lowing for their daily rations of hay or an owl's mournful hoot that made me think it was saying, "Who-who are you?" Mom called the hot August days, the dog days of summer. If a dog was going to get rabies it would happen this time of year. I never understood why June bugs were named for June when they never came until July.

35

As a child I avoided "wasp's nests" and thistles in the pasture. I watched and listened as grasshoppers flew away from under my feet, making a clicking sound. We fished in our pond and caught bullhead catfish we never ate; they never survived the trip to show mom and hear her praise. By the time we returned them to the water it was too late. In the winter when we could see our breath, we knew it was forty degrees, when our nose fluids froze, we knew the temperature was freezing.

I made whistles out of hickory limbs and used tree forks for bean flippers. I was always looking for red rubber from worn out auto tire inner tubes. Tongues from worn out shoes were used to make the flippers. We were also always on the lookout for round rocks because they shot straighter.

Swimming in the pond may not have been hygienically healthy but it sure cooled you off in August.

We had an old International truck that didn't look like much; it was scratched, dented and noisy. The hand-crank windows were difficult to raise and lower. They stayed down unless it rained. Its transmission had four speeds forward. Compound gear was the lowest and strongest gear, used for moving an extra heavy load when off a paved road. Low gear was used for getting a heavy load moving, then at the right speed or momentum, we'd shift into second gear. This gear continued the momentum until an adequate speed was reached and we would shift into high gear. When a steep upgrade was ahead, we downshifted to second gear.

The old transmission was weak and would often slip out of high gear. Dad cut a section of a small board with a notch that fit against the floor gear shift, and wedged against the dash to keep the transmission in high gear. When I was with him, I would be the one to wedge the board against the gear shift and the dash of the truck. When we came to an upgrade that required a down shift, I would quickly remove it. I became good at it; I could tell when it was time to shift and dad didn't have to say a thing. The little board came out and back in when it was time. Dad and I were a team.

The first job I remember my father working included that old International truck. He would buy a stand of cedar trees called a cedar break (A cedar break was a tract of land that contained standing cedar trees of a size perfect for fence posts). Dad hired Charley Tate, for three dollars a day to help him cut. A cedar tree has a hard-red core that will not rot or deteriorate with time. A fence, constructed of cedar posts is almost maintenance free. Dad and Charley would cut the cedar posts with axes and buck saws, haul them to the post yard, and sell them to truckers who trucked them up north to sell to farmers. One time the loaded truck caught fire on the way home, dad burned up his coat but he got the fire out.

Dad always had his gun with him in the woods. Occasionally he would shoot a squirrel or two and bring them home for us to eat. One work day in the timber, he shot a hawk and gave it to Charley Jones who loved to eat them.

Dad followed the wheat harvest in Kansas and would be gone for several weeks but he made good money. He was a good provider for his family.

For me, life was wonderful, but for the nation as a whole, life was a struggle. Reflections on the past fills my mind with family, the Ozark people and culture, and the values and virtues that were instilled into me. The reverence for God, the importance for honesty and fairness when dealing with people are values that I still consider important and continue to live by. I have great pride in being born and raised in the Missouri Ozarks Mountains. God blessed me immensely, allowing me to be born and raised in this section of our nation.

Mombasa Kenya

CHAPTER 6

My Family Moved to Kansas

I was three years old when Hitler invaded Poland in 1939 and World War II began. The US government sent supplies to aid England but avoided direct involvement. In 1941 Japan attacked our naval base at Pearl Harbor, Hawaii which unified our entire nation and changed the course of history. The American President from Missouri, Harry Truman, used a recently developed weapon called the atomic bomb, against Japan which ended the war in the pacific theatre. Later, America declared war against Germany. In 1945, the "D" day invasion was the beginning of the end of the war in the European theatre.

Dad's age and having a family kept him from active military service, but not his involvement in the war effort. In the spring of 1942 my father, mother, Max, age one and I moved.

A large truck, equipped with side boards called stock racks, the kind used when hauling cattle, backed up to our house. Dad, with the help of neighbors, loaded our personal belongings. I thought riding in the rear of a truck on a mattress was a neat way to travel to a new state. We were heading for Kansas. McCune, Kansas was located near the army munitions plant in Parsons where my father worked producing large artillery shells.

There, I experienced my first inside toilet and a coal-burning heating stove. Rabbits were plentiful and we shot them from the front fender of a car at night along a country road. I don't know if it was legal or not but they tasted good. I was too young to shoot but dad took me along.

Children of the town gathered and placed scrap metal at a designated location which was picked up and used to fight the war. I didn't like the air raid drills when all the street and house lights were turned out and we had to go to bed early.

I turned 6 in July of that Kansas year and attended my first grade of school that fall. I usually walked the few blocks to school. I fell in love with my teacher Mrs. Hankens and two girls in my class; I remember Lois, but can't remember the name of the other girl. A magician came to the school and performed in an assembly. He called me up on stage and asked me to drink water out of a cup. He then pulled a white mouse out of the same cup. Everyone laughed at me. It really didn't matter much; I enjoyed the performance.

Almost every day on my way home from school, I detoured a block and walked through downtown. I often would watch two deaf people communicate using hand signs. Mom never even noticed I was a little late getting home.

The cap I wore didn't have a bill and was made out of leather edged with wool that could cover my ears. I didn't like the tassel on top so I tore it off and told mom it came off. I also didn't like to take a thermos bottle to school so coming home one day I fell down on purpose and broke it.

In the early 1940's our family, now numbering five, Cleota had been born in Kansas, returned to the Missouri Ozarks. Back in Missouri, I often watched large convoys of soldiers and equipment pass by our house headed north to perhaps a train station for deployment to a battle zone. I would wave and the soldiers would wave back. War news was scarce since there were few radios or television sets. Most news came from the newspaper or the news reels at movies.

Once at my grandfather's home, we were watching (that is what you did back then), and listening to a large cabinet radio. The reporter talked about two American soldiers returning to base in a jeep. A Japanese solder with a white flag stepped out of the bushes in front of the jeep. They stopped and signaled for him to come on out.

Several Japanese soldiers, wanting to surrender, followed him out. The soldiers in the Jeep instructed them to proceed in a single file down the road. When they entered camp, they made the news. I'm sure the prisoners were later questioned and processed into the confinement facilities.

My school house in the back ground in McCune,
Kansas where I attended my first grade in 1942. This picture
as taken in a 2020 visit

My brothers and sisters
Rick, Lavonna, Cleota, Hobert and Max

CHAPTER 7

The Fleagle Place

We came home from Kansas to our two-room house, but soon Dad bought the house and land next door. This six-room house included our present house and 300 acres of land located on US Highway 65 one and a half miles north of the Arkansas line in Missouri called the Fleagle Place. It has since been altered by a new and improved highway and the old house has long deteriorated and been destroyed. My brothers, sisters, and I still own the land that was once occupied by members of the notorious Fleagle gang, a band of bank robbers. (See appendix C)

That fall I began second grade in a two-room school house. It was unique as it had a belfry with a bell used to call children back to class after recess. A large wood stove was center in each of the class rooms. Men in the community cut wood that was stored near the front of the building. The teacher usually came early and had a fire going before class began. During warm months we children came to school barefoot.

Ridgedale was not really a town, maybe a village, we had our own post office, a school and only two businesses existed. Tommy Curbow's grocery store, which also sold gasoline and supplies needed for cattle, for a season contained the post office. Kohler's store sold groceries and no gasoline and was run by a tiny woman we all called Miss Kohler, she probably weighed less than 100 pounds and loaded sacks of feed with little effort.

43

Shortly after returning home from Kansas in the early 40's, my dad bought a business that was closed. It was an existing gas station, grocery and feed store. Our inventory consisted of almost everything. We could have put up a sign that said, "If we don't have it, you don't need it," which would have described what we had to offer."

I learned all aspects of the business. We fixed flats on both automobile and truck tires. I often patched auto tire tubes, as tubeless tires had not been invented. I would scrape or rough up the tube in the area with the hole that caused the leak. Apply a special cement to the surface area, then using a special clamp, raw rubber affixed to a metal apparatus that contained a material much like the sparkler of today's fireworks that wouldn't flame but just burn slowly. The raw rubber, if all went well, would melt and became part of the tube and would seal the leak. Flats were fixed using two iron tire tools, 30-inch-long tools with paddle like ends, that were inserted between the rim and the tire to separate the tire from the wheel. The tire with patched tube was reinstalled using the same tools and a rubber hammer. Air was then applied to see if the patch job had properly fixed the leak

Unless there was a gas war, I pumped a lot of 15.9 cent gas. The price could also be up to 5 cents lower. We sold a lot of "tailor-made" cigarettes for fifteen cents a pack plus we also sold loose tobacco. Prince Albert, Velvet and Bull Durham tobacco were available if you wanted to roll your own. I liked Bull Durham because it was in a small sack when I was slipping around smoking, I could hide it in the top of my sock, the other brands were in metal cans.

I learned how to meet the public and handle cash to make change, there were no credit cards, it was all cash. The Youngblood station provided full-service when you stopped for gasoline. I would pump your gas, clean your windshield and check the oil and air in the tires. I especially liked it when a customer said fill-it up please. Since our dispensing nozzles were not automatic shut off, I could wedge the gas cap in the nozzle and often have the oil checked and the windshield cleaned and get back to the pump before the tank was full. It was always better when dad and I worked together.

44

We did sell a lot of gasoline. Harp truck-line located in Harrison, Arkansas, bought gas from us for their trucks that hauled freight throughout the Ozarks. Since we were the first business that one encountered out on the ridge, many folks traveling south bought their gasoline in Missouri because of the tax charged by Arkansas.

The village or town of Ridgedale, Missouri still has a post office. The school building is gone and its location is only remembered by us old folks. Ridgedale, Missouri now only exists in the minds of folks like me who grew up there and remember the past. The relocation of US 65 highway now bypasses the old business locations which are nonexistent or vacant. Tommy Curbow's location is now a church.

The Ridgedale zip code (65739) address is still active and now being used by a restaurant called Top of the Rock, a high-end place where you pay for the ambience. A national golf course frequented by top names in the sporting world and Big Cedar Lodge, a prime vacation spot and conference center. The almost 300 acres my family received as an inheritance is for sale.

The 40's were my formative years. My values of truthfulness, honesty, dependability, faith in God, and love of country was all developed by my relationship with family and hill folks that crossed my path. My first job was in the 40's, picking strawberries for Jess Youngblood (my grandfather's brother). A flat of strawberries contains eight quarts and weighs about twelve pounds. I was paid ten cents a quart.

When I received my first bicycle and learned to ride, I rode it around and around the store building. Near the back of the store, I ran over something, fell, hit my left arm on a block of wood and bent it. The doctor said my youth caused my bone to bend and not break. He put a tightly wrapped bandage type of splint on my arm, the swelling went down and the splint became loose, I took it off and have a left arm that is crooked. It is not noticeable but I can't hold that arm straight like the other one.

I learned to shoot with a Daisy Red Ryder BB gun. I could hit pop lids, (the metal kind that were pressed on and not reusable) without a miss. I also could, on occasion, strike match stick. One year the "Jar Flies" (Cicadas) were plentiful and a perfect target for the BB guns. My sister Cleota would wear a little apron and fill it with dead jar flies as we shot them. I seldom missed. Max was also a good shot so her apron filled quickly.

The Ridgedale open air movie theatre had galvanized tin walls that were too low to crawl under and too high to see over. The owner and his wife would come down weekly. Admission was ten cents. We sat on wooden benches on gravel floor and watched black and white, mainly western movies. We boys always wanted westerns, not those love shows that were for girls. Gene Autry, Roy Rogers, Johnnie Mac Brown, Smiley Burnette, Gabby Hayes, Tom Mix, Lash La Rue, Tex Ritter, Andy Devine, William Boyd as Hop-a-long Cassidy and the Cisco kid were all popular cowboys of that era. I don't remember ever seeing a movie with John Wayne back then.

My favorite radio programs were Jack Armstrong, the All-American Boy, The Shadow, The Fat Man, Sky King, and Gang Busters. I learned to play cords on the mandolin and guitar. I had always wanted curly hair so I got a home permanent called a Toni.

Keeping her family healthy was on the top of Mom's list. If you looked a little peaked or moved a little slow, she would prescribe a good dose of cod liver oil to help your bowels move. One day Max was headed for the treatment and trying to stop the inevitable, asked Mom, "What is this stuff for?"

"To make your bowels move honey!" she spoke.

Max, not knowing what bowels were said, "Mom, I don't need it, they are moving now."

It didn't matter how I felt, I always tried to hide it from mother. I avoided cod liver oil at all cost. It is really nasty tasting stuff.

Folks short on money, who were traveling though our area would sometimes offer things for sale when they stopped at our store. In 1948 when I was twelve Dad traded for a twenty-six-inch motorized bicycle called a Whizzer. The Whizzer is a line of bicycles equipped with small gas engines produced in the United States from 1939 to 1965. To get it started the rider would hold in the clutch on the handle bars and pedal like a normal bicycle. When it got up to speed the rider could release the clutch and the momentum would start the engine. The brakes were on the pedals like a normal bicycle.

In 1948 US Highway 65 was black top with very little traffic (partially because in 1942 the auto industry had ceased production on cars to produce military hardware) and I rode that Whizzer everywhere.

My grandparents, who I thought were old at that time, grandpa was fifty-one, and grandma was fifty-six, they always got up early and had a country breakfast: biscuits, gravy, ham, bacon and eggs. So, especially in the summer, to their delight I would hop on that Whizzer and ride the mile to their house. The air was clear and my whizzer bicycle motor that sounded like a bee hive would precede me.

Grandpa Luther would say, "Della, set another plate, I hear Hobert coming."

I always found my plate waiting. Those biscuits, red-eye gravy and fresh meat or bacon hit the spot. My grandma made red-eye gravy by pouring a little coffee in the grease left in the skillet after she fried the meat.

Stray Animals

In my younger years in the Ozarks, it was not unusual to find unwanted stray dogs and cats alongside the road. People dropped unwanted dogs near a house, hoping they would be fed by the people living there. Cats were dropped off near someone's barn. They would survive on rats and mice. At our house neither man nor animal was ever allowed to go hungry. Stray dogs were numerous. My first pet came from that lot. He was a shepherd dog I called King. Though we had other hunting dogs, everywhere I went King was with me. A few years later King left; he just wasn't around. Later I found him partially deteriorated; he had gone into the timber to die because he had contracted distemper.

When I was a young child, maybe four years old, on the way to Harrison, Arkansas, my dad dropped off a little dog near a house with a two-wheel trailer out front. The dog was a mongrel with no value on the farm. As we returned home, I could see the little dog still under that two-wheel trailer and I began to throw a fit and cry. I wanted my dog. My dad didn't pay me any attention and went on home. I put up such a fight that in the middle of the night my dad and I went to find my dog. Sure enough, he was still under the trailer. He came home with us and I finally went to sleep. I don't remember what ever happened to that dog but I got him back.

Another dog from my childhood was Whizzer a medium-size, black-haired, mixed breed that belonged to Grandpa Luther Youngblood. Whizzer was a fast dog. Many times, I would be squirrel hunting with one of my uncles and Whizzer would tree a squirrel. If the squirrel went into a hole in a tree with a rotten center, we had to cut down the tree to get it. When that tree hit the ground, Whizzer would, without fail, catch the squirrel on the ground. These hunts always ended with Grandma Della fixing us a meal of fried squirrel, biscuits and gravy or sometimes squirrel and dumplings. It was worth cutting a tree for.

Grandpa had a Bluetick hound named Ole Blue that spent numerous hours at our house. He was supposed to be a good coon dog, but I don't know if anyone ever took him hunting. Mom would complain that she couldn't feed our dogs because of Ole Blue.

Oil for cars came in metal cans with a special can opener. M-80 firecrackers were not illegal at that time. I took an empty oil can, tied it to Ole Blue's tail, and dropped in a lit M-80 firecracker. Ole blue started dragging that can behind him looking a little puzzled. The firecracker went off and so did Ole Blue. I don't think he touched the ground more than twice as he vacated the premises. Needless to say, he didn't return and mom had no more trouble feeding our animals.

48

Being the first grandchild on my father's side I received special attention from my paternal grandparents (Luther & Della Youngblood) and formed a special bond with my aunts and uncles. I also had a special bond, though different, with my maternal grandparents, George and Victoria Youngblood.

Mom and dad prior to marriage both had the Youngblood name. mother's family was from Kentucky and dad's family was from Oklahoma. They were distant cousins.

Mother's parents often stayed with us when grandpa was preaching revival meetings in the area. Grandpa always wore garters on his shirt sleeves to keep them from covering his hands. I also remember the hat that grandma always wore. Grandma Victoria died in August 1946. She had been living in our two-room house on our property.

Even though I didn't really surrender to God until in my twenties my faith in God became embedded in me from my mother and contact with her brothers and sisters. Grandma Della, dad's mother, also played a major part.

It was during those times I got to know many of my uncles, aunts, and cousins on mom's side. The importance of God was so evident when Uncle Paul and Aunt Hattie and their children, Uncle Bill and Aunt Jessie Wright and their children would come for an extended visit. Uncle Phillip and Aunt Bertha and family moved to the area. Uncle Silva and Uncle Clyde both had family problems and often came and spent extended time with us. Paul and Phillip both had trucks. They bought and sold cedar posts, water melons, and peaches.

When we returned from Kansas my father bought this service station: note the pump on the far end, when there was a power outage it didn't need electricity, gasoline was purchased with this pump in five-gallon increments

Home economics' room in Hollister High, Sherry is on the left.

CHAPTER 8

Hollister High School

It was in May of 1950, at thirteen years old, I sat on the stage of the Hollister School gym, waiting to be promoted into the freshmen class of a new school. My two-room country school was closing and I would be attending high school in Hollister, Missouri. I was the valedictorian of my eighth-grade class and was to give a speech. I don't know what I said (I'm sure my mother said I did a good job), but I do remember a girl, sitting behind me on stage, who was also graduating from the eighth grade. There was no chemistry, no love at first sight. In fact, I was just savoring the moment. But this girl, Sherry McClease, and some of her cousins were seated behind me and, being the new boy in town, I was receiving all the attention from the girls and I liked it.

That fall brought a big change in my life. I went from riding a small van with no windows and two bench seats to an actual school bus, from a class room with ten to twelve students to a high school of sixty people. I had a lot of names to learn. Our school colors, blue and white, soon graced a sweater I proudly wore representing my school. Bells rang between classes and we had more than one teacher. The coach (yes even a coach) showed us how to use special powder in our new tennis shoes we had to wear on the gym floor to control athletes' foot. I learned how to hold a basketball with the tips of my fingers and use my wrists when passing or shooting a basket. We had several flush toilets and real toilet paper.

51

Several of my eighth-grade classmates didn't go on to high school but I made new friends quickly. There were a lot of girls. I mean a lot of girls! I fell in love with Patsy Jones. We had a short romance. We giggled a lot when we saw one another. We tried to walk on the same side of the hall in order to pass as near as possible to each other. I touched her hand once, man I thought, if I only had a car. Being fourteen was a great inconvenience.

The school always presented a junior senior play, which included freshmen and sophomores. I was in the play all four years. In one play, Aunt Samantha Rules the Roost, I had to dress up like a girl on stage and I was so small they picked me up and dropped me into a girdle. The crowd went wild. I don't remember the other plays except that they were a lot of fun and our group became very close.

Our basketball team, the Hollister Tigers, had a pretty good record. In tournaments, we would often place and bring home a trophy and on occasion we would win first place. Going to the games was a big deal. I wasn't much of a basketball player but I kept score. My game was softball. We didn't have a large enough area for baseball. I was first string catcher and a good hitter. I wasn't strong enough for the long ball, but I learned to meet the ball. I was leadoff batter; and often went four for four.

My love for Patsy sort of waned after my freshmen year and Sherry began to catch my eye. She hung out with some of her cousins and word got around to me that she liked me. I put the word out that I kind of liked her, so the romance sparked. We were in plays together, sat together at some of the basketball games and had some classes together. I would get a chair next to her, just so we could talk about the lesson. We became boyfriend and girlfriend, not going steady, mind you, just a level above good friend.

Table manners were something I wasn't particularly concerned about until I came to Hollister School. I began keeping my left hand in my lap and eating with my right hand. It was not very comfortable but I wanted to be proper, especially when other people were around. I worried about balancing my food on a fork while getting it in my mouth.

Sometimes the school would have a special night when a local square dance caller would come and call a dance. They wanted to keep the culture of the Ozarks alive. The cooks would bake a sheet cake to eat during the break. I would concentrate on using a fork to eat that cake and jello. I liked this girl and sure didn't want to make a fool of myself if she were watching.

In my early years living in Ridgedale I seldom went to Branson or Hollister, but when I started attending Hollister High school, my friends, activities and interests shifted to that area. Prior to my sixteenth birthday and getting my driver's license I associated with guys who could drive. Many of my friends were seniors and we would double date.

Chick Miller gave the best flat top haircuts of any one around. Real sodas, cherry cokes, and vanilla shakes were available at the drug store next to Chick's barber shop. My first time at that soda fountain, sitting with three of my school friends having a vanilla shake, I tried to hide that I had never been there before. I was acting nonchalant, talking, and without looking at my glass I started to take a drink and stuck the straw up my nose. There I was, with a straw up my nose, the shake dripping off the straw on the table and my reputation totally ruined.

The Shack served a good hamburger. The pool hall was always smoke filled, and I didn't play pool so I seldom went in there. The Branson movie theatre, a far cry from the open-air theatre in Ridgedale, was always a place to go.

Sherry and I could go to the movie for a dollar. Back then musicals were the going thing. Meet Me in St. Louis, Oklahoma, Singing in the Rain, Annie Get Your Gun, To Kill a Mocking Bird, and Picnic were movies I remember. Fred Astaire, Ginger Rogers, Ray Bolger, Gene Kelley, Debbie Reynolds, Eddie fisher, Bob Hope and Bing Crosby were all movie stars. My favorite girl singers were Doris Day, Teresa Brewer, Patti Page, Rosemary Clooney, Kay Strafford and Dinah

Shore. Men singers were Perry Como, Frank Sinatra, Nat King Cole, Dean Martin, Sammy Davis Junior, and Tennessee Ernie Ford. Later Western movies became popular. Some movies that had a major impact on my thinking were Magnificent Obsession, The Yearling, The Grapes of Wrath and The Jackie Robinson Story.

Arts and Helen's was north of town, a small place with a lot of things that tourists buy. They served a good hamburger and was something different to do. A spot with a reputation was the Skyline, a lot of people would gather there on Saturday night. It was rumored that they sold drugs. I had no interest in trying drugs so I seldom spent any time there. The White Elephant was a combination gas station, restaurant and dance hall. We all would check out the Elephant a couple times a night just to see who was there. I liked their corned beef sandwich and the atmosphere. Sherry liked to dance the jitter bug but I didn't even try to learn. When we would go there, she would often dance with Van Michel. I didn't worry, they were just friends and I was much better looking. I never was much of a dancer but when I did dance, I always preferred slow dancing,

Since few of us had a telephone at home, we would often meet at P junction north of Hollister and plan our evening. On Halloween night we would take a BB gun and shoot out street lights. They had exposed screw-in bulbs. Then we would go trick or treating. Sometimes we would go to Table Rock Lake and try to throw a rock into the river down below. It can't be done but we would always try. If we stopped there to talk, we were joined with other cars. It was a place we would all congregate.

We would drive out to Inspiration Point, a place made famous in the book Shepherd of the Hills by Harold Bell Wright, and just hang out. Sammy Lane's lookout, also mentioned in the book, was a popular place to park and look out over the hills and talk.

Even though we were underage we could usually get our hands on some beer. I was with some boys one night and we got caught with beer by Wayne Ferguson, a state trooper. He did his best to find out who bought the beer for us, but we stuck to our story that we found it. Drinking hard alcohol was rare but occasionally someone would have some old Crow. Over the summer I often would catch for a local softball team and would keep a half pint of whiskey in my ball bag just for looks. During some of the games I would try to chew tobacco, I even poured in some honey to try and make it taste better, but I couldn't pick up that habit.

Often during the summers Sherry and I were separated. I was in California; she was in Arkansas or Oklahoma. Her Dad was a plastering contractor and my father followed construction and we would go where he was working. Sherry and I would date other people. My dates were all just to hang out. Barbara Baughman was easy to be around and a good dancer, Oma Jean McFarland was just a buddy and fun to play catch with, Betty Meadows was nice to talk with and easy to be around, but when Sherry came back the flame would rekindle between us.

One summer I worked in Kansas City for the Hudson Oil Company. On weekends I would drive home, pick up Sherry, put cans of beer in a bucket with ice and go to a drive-in movie. I would be so tired that we never opened a beer, I just laid my head in her lap and slept through the entire movie. We didn't care, we were together.

My freshman year the Table Rock Dam was just in the planning stage. Our Hollister School band dressed in our dark pants, white shirts and ties, and played at the groundbreaking ceremony. A few years later I worked on the construction of that dam. I made one dollar and twenty-five cents per hour and spent it all on Friday night after pay day, going out with Sherry.

When our senior year rolled around, we had ten in our class. Back then the grades were E, S, M, I and F. Wanda Holland led the class with an E average, Sherry had an S+ average and I had an S average. Since our class was small, we were allowed to take a senior trip. We met weekly at one of our homes and made fudge which we sold along with popcorn at basketball games to raise the money.

A few weeks before graduation we set out for the gulf coast, stopping in Nashville for the Grand Old Opry, still in the Old Ryman

Theatre, then on to Gulf Port, Mississippi for time on the beach, and finally to New Orleans and a guided tour of the city. Then we came back home for graduation (May 1954). During this time, it became clear that Sherry and I were meant for each other. We had become more than just girlfriend and boyfriend.

She was the love of my life. Sherry was 18 and I was 19.

CHAPTER 9

A Dear John Letter

Her family, like mine, were poor—but neither of us knew it. Her father, like mine, had to leave the family in the summer for work. She spent much of her young life with her brother, sister, and mother. She played in the hay loft of their barn for hours and rode an old horse. She played with her cousins in a creek that ran through their property, and roamed the hills of their family farm in Taney County, Missouri.

Most of our dates involved my family's first new car that dad purchased after he sold the business. We were especially proud of that car, a green, six cylinder, 1950 Chevrolet Deluxe. He paid Binkley motors in Branson, Missouri $1820.00 for it and received a full tank of gasoline. It was a three-speed shift on the steering column, no turn signals or AC, but it had a heater and an AM radio.

We would laugh and say it had 4/60 air conditioner, all four windows down and going sixty miles per hour there was lots of air flowing in the car. No split seats for me, I wanted my girl sitting right next to me, with my right arm around her, driving with my left hand. Shifting was a challenge, but I managed.

One night we pulled in and parked in front of the Clarence Gentry house where Sherry was staying with her cousin Clarice while her parents were on a trip. It had been a good night. Sherry as usual, was sitting close to me on that bench seat. It was always difficult for us to end our dates; it would be tomorrow before we could see each other again.

"Sherry, I love you"

57

It was a beautiful night, a gentle breeze was blowing, and the car windows were open, providing a perfect temperature. The beams from a full moon filtered down and bathed the front seat of the car with a soft light. As we sat in silence, I looked at her. She was the picture of perfection: a dark blouse, her hair blowing gently in the breeze. I was overwhelmed with her beauty. I wanted to spend the rest of my life with this girl. My words were unrehearsed, they just came out from the very depth of my heart, perfectly expressing my emotions. "Sherry, I love you" I said. Though no date was set, we knew, when the time was right, we would be married. We were seventeen.

After graduation I began working construction on the Table Rock Dam project. My first job was running a number two shovel, adding ship-lap rock treatment to the down side of the dam. A dump truck would bring in a load of stone and with a shovel I, along with the rest of the crew, would spread it in the proper place.

Next, I was assigned to the dynamite crew. Deep holes were drilled in a straight line in the rock bluff with a wagon drill. We loaded the holes with dynamite and set them off, blasting the rock away leaving a clean break in the bluff. The rock was used in the construction process and the cliff was left neat and clean, eliminating falling rock.

Later I hung over the side of the bluff in a rope sling, using a pressure water hose to clean the rock and debris away, preparing it to receive the concrete on the south side of the dam.

That fall we both enrolled in SMS College (now Missouri State University). We didn't have any classes together; academically we went in different directions. I was involved in ROTC, drafting, speech, literature, Spanish, and some general subjects. Some of my academic preparation for college was lacking, therefore part of my first semester classes were subjects my entrance tests found insufficient.

I failed spelling because I was caught cheating on a test. I had broken a pencil into a couple of two-inch lengths and made a scroll using adding machine paper and a rubber band. I could thumb the scroll to the word I needed. I got caught, received an "F" on my paper and never went back to the class.

I excelled in ROTC, usually winning the weekly company inspection by being the best dressed soldier. I would spit shine my shoes, and using brillo pads made my brass shine. You could see your image in them. I did well in speech and Spanish and even with my "F" I had a good enough grade average to not be on probation.

Once I was taking Sherry to a movie called 'pffst' (the sound). It was foggy and I was driving a borrowed Jeep. I hit and actually climbed upon the rear of a Nash automobile and did considerable damage to the left rear quarter. I hired a local man to hammer out the dents and I paid him over the summer.

That following summer I worked in Kansas City and came home on weekends. I started working at a local bakery, the owner wanted me to pull the lawn mower while cutting the grass, and of course I pushed it. After a week that job ended.

Later the Hudson Oil Company hired me as an attendant pumping gas. Every Friday I would work a full shift in Kansas City, drive 180 miles to Hollister, pick up Sherry, get a bucket, ice down our beer, and go to the drive-in movie. We didn't drink the beer because I would go to sleep, my head in her lap. She would watch the movie and wake me when it was over. What a date. We were together as much as possible.

The gas station where I had worked was robbed right after I quit working there.

'Dear John'

With no emails and telephones available, the postal letter was the method Sherry and I used to stay in contact during the times we were separated before we were married. We still laugh about the time that summer when I wrote her a "Dear John" letter, breaking up with her because of another girl I had met. To the best of my knowledge, it went like this:

59

Dear Sherry,

This is not an easy letter to write, nevertheless, it has to be written. We both must go on with our lives and I can't figure out a better way of ending our relationship. It pains me to write this as I don't want to hurt you. I have given much thought about putting my feelings into words, and have concluded that I must at least try since you are such a good person.

Thank you for your friendship and all the good memories we have experienced together. They are things I will keep in my heart forever. I so admire your character, of being real and always truthful. You will never know how much I appreciated the times we have had together. You are all I had ever wanted in a friend. You are always fun to be with and I have always been proud to be with you, in a group with our friends, or when we were alone just listening to music and not talking. I recall the bus rides to basketball games, the Saturday night movies, our visits to the White Elephant, hayrides, and just hanging out at Table Rock. I will always remember.

As Sherry read the first page of the letter her demeanor changed so much that her mother, Lorene, was alarmed and began asking what was wrong. Sherry handed page one to her mom as she continued to read page two. Her mother began to utter her favorite cuss words about me as she read the letter.

Page two contained a description of a little blond headed girl who had captured my heart. I stated that holding her felt so much different than holding Sherry. Her eyes and facial expression captured my attention like no other girl I had ever known. She was cuddly and easy to be with. She just begged you to hold her, and of course I did.

As Sherry continued to read, a teardrop escaped her eye. Her mother wasn't speaking very highly of me either. Neither of them could believe I could throw away a relationship that had been ongoing for the past three years, over some little blond I had met only recently.

I went into detail about how she dressed, smiled, and just generally communicated with me. She had literally stolen my heart. I continued using as many adjectives that I knew to paint a picture of why I had fallen for this other girl. The letter ended abruptly with the very last sentence where I disclosed: she is my cousin and just six months old.

Love Hobert.

Until the very last sentence both Sherry and Lorene had thought the letter was real. At the time it was no laughing matter, had I been where they could have gotten hold of me, I may not have lived. But later we, including Lorene, all laughed about it.
While in Kansas City I was staying with my aunt and uncle Chatty and Junior Dickey. The baby had been born into another family member's home who couldn't care for her and my aunt and uncle, who wanted another child, quickly took her as their own.

Kathy

There were times when Sherry and I were just together, there was little or no conversation, just being together was enough. We would listen to the Tulsa Bandstand, a program that was mostly music. In college we both were busy but often found time between and after classes to talk. We discussed our future, even to the number of children. Ironically, we thought we would have six and picked names for Mark and Steve.

Religion was a subject where Sherry differed somewhat from me. She had joined the Catholic Church at nine years old. She had a special experience with God when she came into the church and was following their rules and regulations; she was at peace and totally confident she was a Christian. My comments that I knew God and believed he existed, but I wasn't yet a Christian confused her. I knew that knowing God existed was different than having a personal relationship with him.

61

Our music had a late thirties, forties and fifties flavor. We listened to the big band era but not much country western. Elvis became popular after we were married. I didn't think he was a big deal. These are a few of the songs we enjoyed and I still like today: Moments to Remember - Four Lads, Unforgettable – Nat King Cole, Star dust – Aerie Shaw, Glow Worm – Mills Bros, Tennessee Waltz – Patti Page, Only You & Harbor Lights – Platters, Hey There – Rose Mary Clooney, Sincerely – McGuire Sisters, You Belong to Me – Jo Stafford

It was a good summer and we both returned to college. I became very disinterested in college and books and began seriously thinking about my future. I had turned nineteen in July and the draft was hanging over my head. I couldn't' make any solid plans, knowing the army could and probably would call me at any time. Though I had enrolled in my second year of college, I decided to enlist and get that obligation over. Without attending a single class, I left college, September 1955, and became Airman Hobert L. Youngblood.

After three months of basic training, I graduated Airman third class from Parks Air Force Base, San Francisco, California. I had orders with a ten-day delay-in-route to report to Francis E. Warren Air Force Base in Cheyenne, Wyoming. Being home with Sherry was great but not long enough. I reported to Cheyenne in the dead of winter. The base was almost vacant and being run with a skeleton crew—almost everyone was home for the holidays. I had nothing to do but stand guard over an empty building. The weather was atrocious. One had to dress like an Eskimo just to go from one building to another. The food in the mess hall was barely cooked. Evidently the guys who knew how to cook were on leave for the holidays.

I was so homesick and discouraged that I called home. "Someone back there has to get sick," I said. "I need to come home." It turned out that Grandma Della was having minor surgery in the doctor's office but that got the job done. The Red Cross called the squadron headquarters and I was issued an emergency leave. Flight control got me aboard a military aircraft in route to somewhere in Tennessee. The plane made an emergency landing in Denver; one of the engines was on fire when it landed. Flight control got me on a second military aircraft with an Air Force General going from Denver to St. Louis. From there I hitchhiked home and went directly to Sherry's house.

We applied for a marriage license. We both had to have blood tests and there was a three-day waiting period. No opposition existed to our marriage, just concern. Sherry's family was concerned that we weren't being married in the Catholic Church. My family had concerns that I was marrying a Catholic girl which would somehow involve me in the Catholic doctrine.

None of those concerns seemed important to me, I wasn't marrying a church organization or a doctrine, I was marrying Sherry McClease, a girl I had known for five years and had dated off and on for four. In the months before our marriage Sherry and I had discussed every aspect of our lives together, including the number of children, where we would live, to our understanding of whom God was and our relationship with Him. This was not a hasty decision. I was confident she was the girl I was supposed to marry. My relationship with my family was good, though at that time, I thought I was much wiser than my parents.

Dad was born in 1911 and Mother in 1915. The great depression had descended on the nation. Dad said, "At that time you couldn't buy a job." They were married in the midst of those times in 1931. The first few years of their marriage times were tough. Dad and mom instilled in all their children a sense of independence and confidence. They supported us fully. Sherry was well received. She and my dad and mom were great friends. In mother's opinion the spouses often were not good enough for her children, but Sherry made the grade. She seemed to be a favorite. I knew I had their full support.

With twelve dollars in our pockets, we were married January 10, 1956 in the living room of a Methodist preacher in Branson,

Missouri. Clyde Noel, a school mate, and his girlfriend were our witnesses. On January 12 my dad helped me buy our first car, a 1948 Chevrolet, for 300 dollars.

Sherry's dad was not in favor of the marriage but when Sherry was getting her clothes from her room at their house, he gave us 100 dollars. My mom went through her kitchen and gave us a house-keeping outfit. On January 14, with everything we owned in the back seat of our car, we started our life together, $300 dollars in debt, in the dead of winter on the road to Cheyenne, Wyoming. Sherry was eighteen, I was nineteen.

We didn't consider our unsure future or the obstacles we would face. Lack of money was no concern. I had a job that would last four years and we would get by. What really mattered was we were together, we had each other. As time went by, we discovered that even though we hadn't given much thought to God and His will, He had been involved. He had loved and protected us and we hadn't even recognized it. Our life together has been a delightful trip. We never talked much when we were together, even on a trip, I would reach over and take her hand, and just the touch is all it took.

Jeremiah 29; 11 For I know the plans I have for you," declares the LORD, "plans to prosper you and not to harm you, plans to give you hope and a future. 12 Then you will call on me and come and pray to me, and I will listen to you. 13 You will seek me and find me when you seek me with all your heart. 14 I will be found by you," declares the LORD,

My Great Grandfather and Great Grandmother
Bill and Bethena Youngblood

Hoby and Sherry

CHAPTER 10

Just Married

So, there we were, driving our 48 Chevrolet on which we owed $300 dollars, headed west to the city of Cheyenne in the dead of winter. Packed in the rear seat of our car were pots, pans, plates,  spoons, and forks, some shower gifts and our clothing. It started to snow near the end of our trip. We slid into an intersection in Greeley, Colorado. In Cheyenne at a gas station a fellow saw the packed car.

"Hey, you guys need a place to stay?" he asked. "Yes." We filled our car with gas and following his instruction we followed him to our first apartment, and Mr. and Mrs. Hobert Youngblood set up housekeeping.

Our landlords were Tiny and Johnny. Tiny was a small, sixty-year-old, very spry lady, married to thirty-year-old Johnny. Our apartment was three rooms in the basement of their home that we entered through a laundry room. It was very cozy and exactly what we needed at the time. These guys took us under their wing and became like surrogate parents. Johnny took me fishing up on the North Platte River. We had a tent and spent the night. I could hear the coyotes howl and the mosquitos tried to carry me away. Can't say I enjoyed the trip, but I enjoyed his effort in making friends and treating me special.

The city of Cheyenne is a mile-high city like Denver, Colorado and Sherry's cooking, especially her cake making, was an adventure.

67

At that altitude, the cake dough would rise, and I mean rise to the point of several pans under the original pan to catch the dough as it spilled out into the oven.

When our landlords went on an extended trip, they relocated their fish tank to our apartment to facilitate our babysitting the fish. I thought a little beer might keep them from missing their owners. Sadly, when the landlords come home all the fish had expired.

The wind was so bad in Cheyenne, the locals had a saying, "Hang a log chain from a tree limb and if it's blowing straight out it's too windy to work." Sometimes we would take a drive on a one-lane country road with the snow piled higher than the car. I don't know what we would have done if we had met another car.

The radio station program always opened with, "It's a beautiful day in wonderful Wyoming," even if the snow was two feet deep and the wind was blowing ninety mph. We really had a great time in Wyoming. I was making seventy-five dollars a week. Once when we had an extra twelve or thirteen dollars. I gave it to Sherry, took her to town, and told her to buy anything she wanted. When she came back, she had spent two dollars for a belt. She brought the balance back to add to our stash.

Several single airmen made our apartment their home away from home. Sherry would cook for them using the food they stole from the mess hall on base. Often, they would bring ice cream which was always good for dessert. Several of we Air Force familles would go to the drive in-movie. They charged one dollar per car. We would pack the car with as many people possible by setting on each other's laps. We would share a large box of popcorn and a gallon of Kool Aid.

I began my teletype machine training in early January. These machines were totally mechanical and very slow, typing only sixty words per minute. They were like a Model A Ford— faithful, if you take it easy and not push it. The keyboard was like a typewriter. As the message was typed a hard copy was produced, with an option to also create a tape. The paper tape was approximately one inch wide and came in a large roll. A total of five holes numbered one, two, three, four, or five, could be punched in any combination. A hole was called a mark and a blank area was called a space.

A test we used to check if the machine was cutting properly was ry-ry-ry the 'R' was holes one, three, five and the 'Y' was two, four. Since a message could be several pages long the operators would type the message on a long piece of the tape and roll it up. When it was sent it was placed in the tape reader and as the tape fed through the reader the message came out on the distant machine.

I learned to take those machines apart and reassemble them. Proper lubrication and adjustment were key to their trouble-free operation. Myriad tiny springs, clutches and contacts had to be adjusted, cleaned and maintained.

I had a strong desire to please and honor my wife. Though I wasn't Catholic or really anything for that matter. I wanted to provide for my wife the best way I could, and since she had married outside of the catholic church, she was prevented from taking the sacrament. I offered to repeat our marriage vows officiated by a catholic priest so she could go to services and take communion.

I met with the Catholic chaplain on base to discuss a new wedding. He indicated since our union was not sanctioned by God or the Church; that in reality we were living in an adulteress manner. Since we had made such an unacceptable choice, he must counsel us before the marriage and that couldn't be until next Sunday. He emphasized that we must not to be late as he would be fasting until after mass and would be hungry when he met with us.

At home I told Sherry about the meeting and she decided to forget it. We were married, we loved each other, and we would move on from there. I continued to feel badly. In a conciliatory manner I explained that there were people that I knew, and had grown up with, who were not Catholics who were good Christians. I knew you could be a Christian without being a Catholic.

I suggested that she begin to read the Bible, the Word of God. Since God had given it to us to live by, He could give her understanding. I felt sure God would speak to her. I got her a Bible and she read it while I was in training. In the evenings, she would tell me what she had read and ask me questions that I couldn't answer. The main thing that she learned was Jesus had brothers. She had been taught that Mary was a virgin for her entire life. God, by his Spirit, began to work with a couple of dumb, honest kids.

After about six months, I became qualified to repair teletype machines and was reassigned to another technical school at Scott Air Force base in Bellville, Illinois, just across the river from St. Louis. I would be in training to repair and maintain cryptographic machines. I was also informed I had been granted a top-secret clearance and could no longer tell anyone about my new job. If asked, I was to say I was a communications machine repairman.

Sherry and her Sister Alba

CHAPTER 11

Another Air Force Technical School

We left Cheyenne with fond memories and our 48 Chevrolet packed with all our belonging. On the way we stopped in Tulsa, Oklahoma where Sherry's parents were living temporarily. Her father, Earl, a plastering contractor, was plastering a large hospital. At our arrival there was no tension, they were glad to see us both and loved that we were coming home. A bed was provided for me to sleep as we had driven much of the night. Earl finished up that day and we all went to their house in Springfield, Missouri.

In Belleville, only a couple of hundred miles from family, we rented a small apartment. Things went fine until bed time, and guess what, no bed! I called the landlord who told me the roll-away bed was in the basement. I brought the bed up to our apartment but there was no place to keep it but the closet. Can you imagine a couple of kids being so dumb? We actually rented an apartment with no place to sleep. I can't imagine it, but we did.

The landlord refused to refund our money so we stayed there the first month and then moved to Freeburg, Illinois where some of my classmates lived with their wives. The large building contained several apartments, all the ground floor ones were taken. We rented a four-room apartment in the attic. The entrance was through a storage room filled with items.

We spent that 1956 Christmas at home with our families and brought Sherry's sister Alba and my brother Max home with us for a short visit. As usual Mom sent us home with food. Dad had killed a hog and we set out with a large cured ham. The trip went well until we reached St. James, Missouri, south of St. Louis. A large bang indicated the motor had thrown a rod. We left the car there and hopped on the

71

bus for St. Louis, planning to take a taxi home from there. The bus passengers couldn't figure out the strange odor coming from the box Max was holding on his lap. We made it home and ate lots of ham. Sherry's dad sent us sixty dollars so I had the motor overhauled and we continued using that 48 Chevrolet.

After finishing the technical school at Scott AFB, I received orders to report to Arlington, Virginia where I was now assigned to the headquarters communication squadron in the Pentagon. We left Illinois in April 1957; Sherry was eight months pregnant. We had instructions to stop every hour and get out of the car to walk around.

The trip went fine. When we arrived, we rented a motel room, bought a paper, and began our search for our next home. The first day brought no results and I decided if we didn't find a place the next day, I would have enough time to take Sherry home and make it back to base and live in the barracks. But we found a nice place in Alexandria, Virginia just outside of Washington D.C. It was upstairs in the home of an older couple. Mark was born while we lived there. Within a couple of months, a nice garage apartment, belonging to this same couple, became available and that was our home for the next three years. During the time we lived there, due to the distance, we only made it back to Missouri one time to show off Mark. Both our parents visited us there in Virginia—I think just to see Mark.

For someone like me, born and raised in Ridgedale, Missouri, a small community on US highway 65, a two-lane road with a post office, a couple of gas stations that also sold groceries, and a liquor store near the Arkansas state line, Washington D.C. was a shock. Freeways went every which way. I was driving my standard shift on the column, six cylinder, 1948 Chevrolet. I was over an hour late getting home my first day at work. I couldn't cross all six lanes to get to my exit with my low-power engine. Once I'd missed my road, I couldn't find any way to turn around. After what felt like a hundred miles I got headed back in the right direction and everything looked different that way. When I finally made it home, I realized I wasn't in Ridgedale anymore.

The Pentagon has 200 acres of lawn, 8,770 cars parked in sixteen lots, 131 stairways, nineteen escalators, 3,705,793 square feet of office space, 4,200 clocks, 691 water fountains and 284 rest rooms. The people who work there daily consume 4,500 cups of coffee, 1,700 pints of milk and 6,800 soft drinks, prepared or served by a restaurant staff of 230 persons and dispensed in one dining room, two cafeterias, six snack bars, and an outdoor snack bar. *[Info taken from internet]* I was like the farmer who visited Carnegie Hall. He walked in, looked around, and said, "Man, this would hold a lot of hay."

I had a Picture ID that got me into the building. A second Picture ID gained me entrance to the communications center, where the machine operators worked. I had to be recognized by one of my co-workers to enter the crypto equipment maintenance area. The phones were always unplugged, only a flickering light told us we were receiving a call. All schematics and drawings were classified top secret and covered when unauthorized personnel were present. Even though a top-secret clearance was required for my work, all information was on a need-to-know basis. I was not allowed to wander about looking at anything I wanted. If a machine was failing or garbling its message, I could read the message in order to diagnose the problem.

The center was covered 24/7. I liked the evening shift because traffic was light going home, I could wear fatigues, and I encountered fewer officers to salute. Much of the time I worked the midnight shift and slept during the day. For long periods I hardly saw the sun, one time I went to give blood and was told that I needed it more than they did.

In the pentagon the threat of an attack was always part of my thoughts. Our evacuation route was directed by whatever part of the

73

building we were in. My route would be north up the coast, not in the direction of my family. Since I had our only car, Sherry's only option would have been to take the baby and hope someone would pick them up. We were regularly briefed what to do in case of an emergency. Often, according to the messages I saw, there were sightings of soviet submarines off the coast.

I decided early on that I was getting out when my time came. My promotions came on time until the last one; they withheld it unless I would reenlist. No way! Normally I would not have stayed at the same duty station as long as I did. We had just had a new baby and Sherry was pregnant with Steve when my rotation came up the first time, and at the second one, I didn't have enough time left in the service for the rotation period so I stayed at my current duty post.

We didn't make enough money to effectively sustain our family, so on my time off I worked for a janitorial company who had the contract to clean the offices of Fort Belvoir, Virginia, an army base near our home. I made a dollar twenty-five per hour which accumulated to be enough so we could have a nice Christmas. We were very happy, things were good.

On May 1, 1957, in an old wooden barracks building that housed the Fort Belvoir base hospital our first son, Mark, was born. It was a twenty-minute drive. The pains were three minutes apart when we arrived. The nurses were very nice. They took Sherry into an exam room and told me it would be a while before the birth and sent me home with the promise of a call when the event happened. I drove home and the phone was ringing when I walked in. We had a new baby boy. I turned around and retraced my steps, arriving about the time the baby was presentable. Sherry looked great, the baby was red, wrinkled and kind of ugly, but he was ours. I think I got to hold him.

The trip to the base was one I made often because of my job with the janitorial company but I got lost coming home that night. My mind just wouldn't work right, I didn't know where I was or when to turn, I was the father of a son.

As we took Mark home, they gave me a bill for ten dollars and fifty cents. It should have been seven dollars. The extra three fifty was for a test to make sure that Marks blood was normal. It was fine we had a healthy baby. Seventeen months later Steve was born in the same hospital. It was then a modern, brick, multistory building, his cost was seven dollars. At that point we had a total of seventeen dollars and fifty cents in children. I'm told that girls cost more!

I first noticed the change in my thought process when I was heading west with my new bride. The way I was processing information pertaining to life was changing. I suppose some would call it maturity or responsibility. No longer was I concerned with listening to the latest hit song, how I did my hair—I did have some at the time—or making sure I was wearing the latest style in clothes. No longer were we the center of our universe, we now had a son. Another human being had entered the world and was living at our house. I was responsible for him. Sherry and I together had caused him to become a reality. Though I didn't think it could, my love and affection for Sherry increased as I watched her perform as a mother and walk the narrow line of caring for our son and never allowing her husband to feel neglected. I had purpose for everything I was doing.

It was with joy, as Sherry and I, bought groceries to provide food, shelter and clothing for our family. I became concerned for a safe environment; even the package of suckers in the glove compartment had flexible U shape handles that wouldn't hurt Mark if he fell with a sucker in his mouth.

From the very first, Mark was an individual. He had a temper. When he was mad or upset, he would hit his head on the floor. I watched my father, who had come to our house from West Virginia,

75

often put his hand under his head. Mark never really hurt himself, he was just getting attention.

After a year in Washington, DC, we planned a trip home. My father who had been working at construction in West Virginia came up and rode home with us. It was good to be home, but we were ready to return and finish our obligation to the military. We were having trouble sleeping, so we got up at four a.m. and left without saying goodbye to anyone. That sort of got us in trouble. Traveling with our one-year-old son was an adventure. We stopped at a restaurant for breakfast, Mark was fussy because he was hungry. The waitress brought him a cracker to munch on while we waited for our food to be prepared. Mark became rather indignant. He cried out, No! He didn't want a cracker he was "hungee on a plate," hungry on a plate. Mark survived and we returned to our temporary home until my military obligation was fulfilled.

The couple who had been renting the apartment that we moved into, gave us our first pet, a parakeet. The bird had the full run of the house and only slept in the cage at night. He often perched on Sherry's shoulder or on the side pieces of her glasses. But with a new baby the bird became a sanitary problem.

Sherry gave the bird to the new couple who took our old apartment upstairs. One day without thinking the lady opened the door and went outside without realizing the bird was on her shoulder and off it went.

Sherry's dad always had cars with automatic transmissions and she had to learn to drive a stick shift. With Mark laying on the front seat of our 48 Chevy she would drive in circles on a large open field near our house stopping and starting, using the clutch, shifting from low to second and then into high gear. It was very nice that she could share the driving on long trips. I have a picture of her changing a tire on the car. She learned how to jack the car up using the cross wrench to loosen the lug bolts on the wheel and change a flat tire.

When we first arrived in Washington the air force took us on a site seeing tour of Washington, DC. We visited George Washington's home at Mount Vernon in Fairfax County, Virginia, all the monuments, the Smithsonian, Arlington cemetery and the tomb of the Unknown Soldier. The changing of the guard was an experience. Later when the cherry trees were in bloom, I visited the reflection pool at the Washington monument and took a lot of pictures. Other than those trips we didn't visit much around the area. We were now a family and just settled down, enjoyed life, and worked. Mark's first trip in the car was a visit to the Washington monument.

I became interested in photography while there in Virginia. I spent a lot of money at the time, 100 dollars for a Retina camera; it was the best 35 mm camera that Kodak made short of a professional. A light meter recorded the ambient light around the subject, by turning the knob to the number and then adjusting the lens aperture and shutter speed. The camera produced excellent pictures. My first picture was a giant Canna flower in the front yard of the residence where we lived. I still have it.

Most of our colored pictures were slides that required a projector to view. I usually used Kodachrome slide film with a 10 Asa rating. Projecting the slides on a large screen produced a clear and quality picture that wasn't grainy. All black and white film required chemicals to develop the negatives in a dark room. The negatives were then projected on a special paper and developed, resulting in prints.

Richard Layton, Sherry's cousin, Barbara's husband, was also in the Air force and loaded film into cameras mounted on the air plane used for reconnaissance. He kept me supplied with 35mm black and white film. I would go into our closet and load it into the small cassettes that fit in my camera, and then shoot away. Sherry and I learned how to develop and print black and white photos in the bath room. Photography became a large part of our lives during that time.

I installed an antenna on the roof of our garage apartment, bought a short-wave radio, and listened to radio broadcasts from around the world. Our television, a portable black and white set, became our entertainment. The programs most interesting were senate hearings. Jimmy Hoffa, a union Labor boss, was being investigated for racketeering. Chet Huntley and David Brinkley were the newscasters most watched at the time.

Some of our favorite shows were: The Today Show, The Ed Sullivan Show, The Jack Benny Program, The Honeymooners, What's My Line, The Lawrence Welk Show, The George Burns and Gracie Allen Show, Maverick and big band director Xavier Cugat, his wife and singer Abbe Lane. Rosemary Clooney, Nat King Cole and Perry Como all had variety shows we enjoyed.

On my way home one evening a lady came running out of her house, telling me that her husband was very sick, and had been shot. I didn't go into the house with her but called the sheriff. It turned out the guy had been shot with a shot gun. I was questioned by the sheriff and told my brief story and never heard any more about it. Along that same road I once found an empty money bag. I turned that in to law enforcement.

CHAPTER 12

Honorably Discharged

Seventeen months after the birth of Mark, Steve was added to the family. I had fulfilled my obligation to the United States Military, my time was up, and we were headed home for good to begin life anew. Cleota, my sister, had married while I was in the service and was living in upstate New York. At that time, she was pregnant with their first child and she rode home with us for her first visit.

Sherry and I were returning different than when we left. I had a new outlook on life. With no particular plans for the future, I was at peace knowing that everything, whatever it was, would be alright. I couldn't put my finger on it but things were changing. Something new was happening to me. The air smelled better as we crossed the Mississippi River and re-entered Missouri.

We settled in Springfield, Missouri. The first few months we lived in a small house located on the farm in Greene County that Sherry's parents had purchased. Kraft foods had just opened a creamery and I wanted so much to work there. Putting in applications and numerous follow up visits didn't land me that job.

My first job was a service station attendant doing minor mechanic work, brakes, and tires. The management's dishonesty was a problem so I quit. Next, I worked for a carpenter who was building a house. I lasted a week then I got fired. I just wasn't cutting it.

Filling out applications and actually forgetting where I had applied was my method of searching for work. So, seemingly out of the blue, in the fall of 1959 the telephone company called me for an interview. I was hired on the spot and told to report the next day for a position of an unlocated lineman.

We purchased our first house, located on Irving Street in Springfield, Missouri within a few months of returning. We paid $5,000. Sherry's dad gave us $500 dollars for a down payment so we had a mortgage of $4,500 and a house payment of $78.00. The house had four large rooms, a kitchen, living room, dining room, bed room, a lean-to on the back—which we turned into an extra bedroom—and a screened in back porch.

CHAPTER 13

Southwestern Bell Telephone Company

I was a total novice telephone man with no idea what the job entailed. Needing to climb a telephone pole didn't enter my mind I don't remember being told what the pay was. I had a family and needed a job, so I thought, just show me what to do and I'll do it.

My first assignment on the line crew was "a grunt." I worked on the ground and assisted the men on the pole. My unlocated line crew did most of the construction projects in the small towns outside of the Springfield area. I learned that my salary, with no overtime was $37.50 per week.

Southwestern Bell Telephone (SWBT) furnished everything I needed including the truck and all the climbing equipment: the belt, hooks, lag wrench, and safety equipment. My climbing belt on which all my tools were attached was another story. They gave me a temporary climbing belt, previously used by former lineman until my special order came in. I weighed 150 pounds when I began working for the SWBT; the temporary belt was much too large. I placed pins (wooden pins with threads, on to which glass insulators were installed, to insulate the wire attached to the cross arms) in my back pockets to hold the belt up when I climbed a pole.

Finally, after several days my specially ordered pole climbing equipment arrived. It was the right size and I was off and climbing. The adjustable safety belt clipped into the 'D' rings on either side of the belt in front. This safety belt when placed around the pole, allowed the worker to lean back, freeing both hands to perform the tasks on a pole. There were no bucket trucks available, all aerial work was performed standing on a pole.

I provided my personal clothing including Carhart overalls and boots with a metal plate suitable for climbing poles. Using pole climbers when working on a pole requires the entire weight of the body to be supported on the arches of the feet on a two-inch piece of metal. Special foot wear is required to distribute body weight properly. I purchased a pair of climbing boots containing steel plates built into the soles from "Bone Dry Shoe Company" by mail from the Joplin, Missouri area. I stood on a piece of paper and Sherry drew a picture of my feet, and we sent the drawing and a check to the boot company. When the boots arrived, they fit perfectly and my life of climbing telephone poles became bearable.

My Accident

One day near the beginning of my time with the phone company I stood at the base of a telephone pole, my shirt torn, my chest bloody with several creosoted splinters embedded in my flesh, and a dilemma: what was I going to tell my boss? Southwestern Bell stressed safety above anything else. There were prescribed methods to safely ascend and descend a telephone pole from which I had deviated.

The correct procedure, after finishing the assigned work, was to remove the safety strap from around the pole and with both hands on the pole walk down looking at the pole below for obstructions. My descent began with the safety strap still around the pole, with my arms crossed in front of me. I would lean forward slightly, the safety strap would fall down, then I would walk down never touching the pole with my hands. I repeated this procedure until I was on the ground. Except, it didn't work this time.

I was a young father and husband with responsibilities for a wife and two little boys. I needed the job. I felt a lot of pressure to do everything right and please my employer, so I lied! My explanation to my boss was that when I descended the pole my hooks possibly hit a tack or nail put there by someone advertising a garage sale or perhaps a politician displaying a hand bill. This story was believable but I knew it wasn't the case at all, safety rules required that both hands must be used to descend a pole.

James 1:2-3 (NKJV) 2. My brethren, count it all joy when you fall into various trials, 3. knowing that the testing of your faith produces patience.

This occurrence in my life ends in victory and an important lesson learned.

The ending begins when I called my boss and asked his forgiveness for my lie to him. Next, I had a prayer meeting with God seeking his forgiveness.

Sherry was able to extract all the splinters with tweezers, except one that was large and deeply embedded in the pectoral muscle of my chest. What was I going to do? I had no health insurance, no money for a doctor, just enough to provide for my family. I had called my boss and asked for forgiveness for deceiving him, and made things right with God, so now what?

The teaching of anointing with oil came to mind so Sherry and I anointed me with oil and nothing seemed to happen. I remembered the story of Naaman who dipped seven times in the Jordan River before he was healed so we prayed seven times each time anointing me with oil. We didn't know much about the oil and learned later that olive oil was often used as it was natural and unrefined. We didn't have anything in the house but Philips 66, 3-in-ONE oil so that is what we used.

The Sunday evening church services at Cedar Valley ended as usual; anyone needing prayer came up and sat on the knee-altar and folks would gather around and lay hands on each one and pray. I was first in line for prayer. When they had finished praying for me, I got up and joined the people and began praying for others. As I did, I felt a tingling sensation in my arm down to my chest.

When we arrived home after church, as Sherry was putting the children to bed, I ran a tub bath. We had no shower. If I took my bath at night the next morning I could stay home longer before I had to leave for work. When I undressed and got into the tub, I noticed a large two-inch-long splinter lying on my chest. I called Sherry to come. We knew this was the splinter we had been unable to remove Friday evening when I had come home from work. We also knew we had been the recipient of a miracle. This splinter that couldn't be extracted with tweezers had miraculously come out of my chest, seemingly by itself.

This story illustrates an attitude that is pleasing to the Kingdom of God. Somehow, we hadn't panicked, we had just gone about our business, not knowing what to expect yet expecting everything to turn out alright. The lesson found in James chapter 1 is: God uses the everyday happenings in our lives and turns them into spiritual growth. We must (*My brethren, count it all joy when you fall into various trials*) allow patience to keep our faith from wavering. We must understand that God is in control of our lives. We must stay the course and continue to do what is right as we serve God. As we must count it all joy and rejoice for an attribute called patience to become imbedded in our spirits. When we allow patience to control our actions God can form in us 'perfection, maturity, and completeness' (*all these words have the same meaning*)

James 1:2-4 (NKJV) 2 My brethren, count it all joy when you fall into various trials, 3 knowing that the testing of your faith produces patience. 4 But let patience have its perfect work, that you may be perfect and complete, lacking nothing.

CHAPTER 14

Promoted to Management

I gained valuable experience in every aspect of the outside telephone plant: I set the poles, installed and spliced the cable, and installed telephones in homes. I learned that a pole had to be set to a minimum depth using a "birth mark," a ten-foot stamp on the butt or larger end of the pole, and that the depth of the hole into which the pole was set is determined by ten percent of its height plus two feet. Thus, a thirty-foot pole is buried five feet. A lineman could walk up to a thirty-foot pole and with a quick sight check of the birth mark, which should be about eye level or five feet above the ground, determine if the pole had been properly installed. Also, the lines were designed so a pole would only hold the weight of wire or cable; any side-to-side pull was offset with a down guy or anchor. My crew installed telephone cables on poles in the air and in underground conduit that connected manhole to manhole. Buried cable was usually plowed in by an independent contractor using a dozer and backhoe.

Later in my career I spliced the cable both in the ground, in a manhole and on a platform in the air. A tent could be installed in the air over the work area if needed due to weather conditions. Splicing underground cable (telephone cable installed in a man hole) required a special set of safety rules. No open flame was permitted in a manhole in order to prevent explosion from gas that might collect underground. Fresh air was pumped continuously into the hole while

85

it was occupied by workmen. We kept a special ampule with us that would turn blue if poisonous gas was found or entered our work area.

Maintaining the continuity of the outside sheath was the goal in all of the aerial, underground and buried cables, therefore they were all maintained under air pressure. If the outside covering of the cable, called a sheath, was compromised dampness could enter resulting in a service interruption. An opening in the cable after the splice is complete, is closed using a combination of a special cloth, rubber tape and a soldered lead sleeve. When properly done the telephone cable will hold air pressure eliminating the entrance of water.

In the 1960s the open wire pole line was universally used for both local and long-distance services. Presently most long-distance services are buried or satellite. Currently most rural telephone service now uses smaller cable replacing open wire.

The insulation on a single wire that made up the large multi-pair cable determined the splicing method. The twist-and-sleeve method was used on the wires insulated with a paper covering. Each wire twisted together and soldered, then covered with a small wax sleeve to keep them from touching.

With the advent of the (PIC) plastic insulation cable, splicing was affected by using a small "B" connector, a small plastic-coated connector with teeth on the inside. Using a special tool, called a nico-press, proper pressure was applied to each connector insuring proper connection. This method required two operations to splice a pair of wires. Working with a local machine shop I redesigned a Nico-press; with my innovation only one squeeze of the tool connected two sets of wires saving time

These "B" connectors came in a five-inch cube box that contained 500 connectors. The accessibility of the connectors to the work area was always a problem as they were easily spilled. I designed a sheet metal container that would hold a box of the connectors. To that box I then fastened a half round piece of metal that fit around the knee. I added an elastic adjustable strap that secured the entire

86

contraption to splicer's leg and "voila" the connectors were always at the fingertips. My boss had several made for distribution to all the cable splicers. The invention was named the "Hoby box."

Using the bid system, I moved within the company from my unlocated lineman position to the cable department and worked as a cable splicer's helper where most of my work was in the greater Springfield area and then I became a full-fledged cable splicer.

Working in the cable department was fulfilling but I was occasionally loaned to the cable department in St Louis where I would work with other crews in manholes splicing cable around the clock to finish a job that was too large for the resident splicers. These assignments usually lasted two to three weeks.

Desiring to stay local I moved to another department and began to work as a residential telephone installer. My responsibilities as a telephone installer took me to an average of five to seven residences per day. The black phone was standard and for a fee a colored phone was available. SWBT introduced a new program and began offering five new colors for a onetime charge of ten dollars. I quickly became top salesman out of twenty installers. I would bring in a colored phone, usually ivory, and place it where the new phone would be when the installation was complete.

My question, as I was finishing the installation was, "Is this color ok, or would you rather have something different?" It was not unusual for me to also sell and install the second extension phone and it be colored also.

Occasionally, A person would say, "The black one talks just as good as the colored one."

My response was, "You could put a light bulb in a mason jar and it would shine, but a nice lamp looks much better, just as does this colored phone."

"Ok, you are right, go ahead and leave it," was the usual reply.

The standard question when other installers called in a completed order was, "How many phones has Hoby sold today?" My sales ability gained me name recognition.

Sherry strongly encouraged me to continue my college education by attending night classes. I enrolled at Drury School of Business, a College in Springfield, and installed telephones by day and went to college at night. Majoring in Business Administration I needed only one course for a business degree when I was promoted to management.

My career in management began in the latter part of 1968 when I was promoted to Plant Foreman in Hannibal, Missouri. My crew was responsible for installing and maintaining residential and business telephone services in Hannibal and two smaller towns of Frankfort and Center, Missouri.

Sixteen months later I was promoted to Wire Chief in Kirksville, Missouri. I supervised a plant foreman, plus all the central office personnel. My responsibilities included local service for three other towns plus Kirksville, and a total of thirty-nine towns for long distance service.

CHAPTER 15

Family Life

I believe that God heard our conversations about the number of children we wanted and gave us what was in our hearts. Samuel Mark's and Jeffery Steven's names were both chosen several months before a date for our marriage. I had no problem with the name Tracy Lynn. The rub came with the birth of Susie. I was adamant she would be Susan Ann and announced to our family the name I had chosen. I was at work when the nurse brought the birth papers to be filled out and Sherry filled in the name she wanted, Susanne Kay. A heated argument ensued and Sherry said very sweetly, "I like that name. I chose what she would be called and that is that." It just so happened that Kay, my wife now, which was about 13 or 14 at the time, was our babysitter, and Sherry liked the name Kay so Susie was named after her.

Later on, we had two more children, both girls. When the subject of names came up, I said, "You just name them, you will anyway." So, Julie Gaye and Shelley Layne are what she called them.

We both loved our children and made every effort to help them succeed. We were always sensitive about treating each child the same. When I was on assignment for Southwestern Bell, the company would keep us in a nice hotel and our crew would work round the clock until we were finished and then I would return to Springfield. My suitcase always contained a special gift for each child.

Birthdays were a little different. The birthday child received the cake but every child received a gift. I have a saying that they laugh about but it does the trick, "You are one of my most favorite children." My grandchildren hear the same statement and know that I love them all equally.

When I was busy working for the telephone company and attending night school at Drury School of Business, I would often call and tell Sherry I was on the way home and she would have my bath water prepared so I could go directly to the bathroom, clean up and still get to class on time.

I was notorious about not really listening to Sherry as she caught me up on daily household news. I was totally comfortable that she could handle the home and I would just bring in the paycheck. The special needs of our children were always her top concern, mine also, but not to the extent of Sherry's. She felt they needed new beds. I agreed, but didn't consider it a priority, it was something we would have to take care of later. I came home one day and she had advertised a yard sale, emptied our basement of odds and ends, and also sold all the children's beds. They had no place to sleep that night. I found a company that furnished motel equipment and bought six new beds and mattresses so we could put them to bed. They were sure nice beds, and she was happy. She sure knew how to get my attention.

When we moved from Hannibal to the Kirksville, Missouri area, we first lived on a 640-acre farm near Hurdland. We rented the house but could hunt anywhere on the property. I often took my sons and occasionally the older girls hunting. We hunted rabbits, squirrel, quail and pheasant. I usually had at least one dog that would hunt. A railroad was located on the edge of the property and we often hunted rabbits along the tracks. The school at Hurdland, Mo. allowed Mark and Steve to take their shot guns to school and put them in the teacher's closet: they would hunt the railroad tracks on the walk home after school. They often brought home a couple of rabbits that Sherry cooked for our evening meal.

There were outbuildings, including a barn and a chicken house on the place; we had a few chickens and ducks. Shelley was just walking good and still talked dutchy when she came in one morning and said, a 'kunk (skunk) is eating my chicken. I went out to the chicken house and sure enough she had walked in on a skunk that had killed and was eating a small chicken. I shot the skunk.

Our family grew in number pretty fast. Sherry and I were twenty when Mark was born and thirty when Shelley was born. Mark, May 1957, and Steve, November 1958, were both born in Virginia while I was in the Air Force. The four girls were born while we lived on Irving Street in Springfield, Missouri, Tracy, September 1961, Susie, December 1962, Julie, March 1965 and Shelley, May 1967

Making sixty-two dollars per week forced us to plan to have enough money for food and bills. Every dollar in overtime money on our check went to buy extra groceries. We purchased canned goods by the case when possible. Bologna could be purchased unsliced in three-foot-long sticks; we usually bought two at a time, cut them into manageable sizes, and put the extra in the freezer. We bought a deep freeze from a locker plant through which we could also buy groceries at a discount.

Sherry was excellent at running our household and making our meager earnings stretch to unbelievable distances. She made sure everything was used and nothing was wasted. Maybe at first, Sherry hadn't been my mother's pick as a wife for me, but after watching Sherry manage our household, all my mother had for Sherry was praise.

My mother once described a woman who could waste more with a spoon putting food in the garbage than her husband could bring in with a scoop shovel. That sure didn't describe my wife. Mom and Sherry became great friends and were together often.

My mother used to tell the story that once Sherry was making a pan of brownies for our family and mother assumed because of the size of the pan that Sherry was making plenty for later.

"Do your children like cold brownies?" my mother asked.

"I don't know, Bonnie," Sherry said. "They have never tasted any that were cold."

She purchased a week's supply of day-old bread at the bakery outlet store and froze part of it. Raw hamburger came in a wax-covered, fifty-pound box. We turned making hamburger patties into a family affair. We all gathered around the table, patted them out, and wrapped them in Saran Wrap for the freezer.

We purchased chicken in case lots of twenty-four whole chickens per case, usually a couple cases at a time. We then wrapped them individually for the freezer. Sherry would thaw out a chicken, cut it up, and fry it for our meal. As the family grew in number and stature it was not unusual to serve four chickens per meal.

My father and mother were good as gold but they didn't  relate to my younger brother Rick's generation and he wasn't doing well, so he came to live with us. Our oldest son Mark, was two years younger than Rick who was eighteen years younger than I. He fit right in and became another son which further increased our grocery bill. A loaf of bread wasn't sufficient for a single meal and drinking a gallon of milk per day was not unusual and sometimes we used more than a gallon. Harry Mansfield, the grocer, was always happy to see us come in and watch us leave with multi carts of food.

A few years later, Rick married and returned to south Missouri and later to Branson where in his retirement he drives a tram at Silver Dollar City.

The advent of the microwave oven brought a major change to our family. Pizza, ham, egg sandwiches, and pumpkin pie was prepared in large quantities and frozen in plastic wrap. The children could take a sandwich, a piece of pie, or a slice of pizza, microwave it, and have a snack. Our children had lots of friends with whom they were very generous with food from the deep freeze.

We had a small outbuilding we called a garage even though it was too small for a car. It became a tool shed, storage area, and play area. Mark and Steve bent many nails as they built go carts. I completed our back-yard picket fence by adding on from the corner of the house to the front side of that building. I built it so that one section could be removed if we needed to drive into the back yard.

In cold weather I hung a butchered deer carcass from the rafters to prevent cats and other animals from getting to it. Sherry would go out and cut off a ham or other section as we needed the meat. The carcass would sear over and not a fly or anything would bother it.

The outbuilding had a flat roof on which the children were not supposed to climb. One day Sherry had to leave for a few minutes and Mark or Steve put up a ladder and they both climbed up on the roof. Mark climbed down and removed the ladder. Steve got caught and was in trouble when Mom came home.

The toys and gifts we bought for our children were usually for hands-on projects. When my boys received carpenter sets with small hand saws a mature peach tree growing in the backyard that produced peaches lost its life. When I returned home from work my sons met me so excited. Using a small hand saw, they had worked hard most of the day and cut the peach tree down. It was quite a feat. I would have rather it hadn't happened but I praised them for a job well done. They were so elated with their accomplishment; I just didn't have the heart to say or do anything but act happy. I was very proud of them for their hard work.

As I taught them to throw and catch, a ball would often hit the house, breaking a siding board. The Irving Street house had a back room added after the original house was built. This room had siding I call shiplap. The boards were slightly beveled and narrow, four or five inches wide, made from cedar. The damage wasn't visible from the street so repairs were not a priority. I'm sure at Sherry's direction I finally made the needed repairs.

The back yard was kid friendly and fully fenced, so we knew where our children were at least most of the time. Although once a neighbor came leading little Shelley, still in diapers, home. She had decided to leave home.

I brought home a discarded telephone pole we had changed out. I cut the pole into three posts that were 10ft in length. I buried two of the posts two feet in the ground, placed the other across the top, on which I hung a porch swing. When the children went to bed Sherry and I spent many of our evenings on that swing, enjoying the night breeze, watching the stars come out, and sharing how much we loved each other and how good God was to us.

The family wash was a full day's job using the ringer washing machine. We watched for sales at Sears and purchased a new automatic washer. I plumbed a special pipe so the water from the washer would drain into the floor drain in the small basement. We were so excited that when it was installed, we took chairs down to the basement and sat and watched the machine go through all its cycles.

The same day it was installed Sherry backed our station wagon into a telephone pole and bent the bumper. For several months whenever we would see a car with a bent bumper we would laugh and say, "They just got a new washing machine."

Near the basement door and the new washer, I constructed a clothes line using two four-inch metal posts, with two-inch metal cross pieces. I stretched discarded telephone steel wire taken from the scrap bin on which the washed clothes would be hung. These posts were secured with concrete allowing the wire to be stretched tight enough that no prop was needed to keep the washed clothes from sagging and touching the ground. Those five lines made it so nice to just take the clothes out of the machine and hang them up to dry.

Orville and June Piette were our next-door neighbors in Springfield. He worked as a mechanic on trucks that hauled food stuff. He brought us a large discarded tire that had been used on earth

94

moving equipment. I placed it under the walnut tree in the back yard and filled it with sand. Our children used it as a sandbox.

The children also wanted a dog. We got a shepherd puppy, that at the time, was small enough to get out of the back yard by going between the pickets in the fence. That quickly changed. On hot summer days the dog would crowd the children out of the sand box. The children would come to get their mother to move the dog, so they could play in their sand box. He became so large we later gave him to a farmer. I'm sure he was happier living in the country.

I moved my family to a larger house on Market Street in Springfield, Missouri that had a basement, Mark and Steve were now boy scouts. When it was pinewood derby time, we went to our basement to prepare the cars we had purchased at a craft store. Using a wood rasp, we filed off the corners to eliminate drag. A small hole was drilled in the bottom of each car and filled with liquid solder which added weight on the bottom of the car. Each wheel was reamed out with a drill bit, that was just the size of the hole to prevent drag. We painted each one a different color, as best as I could, I made sure that they were equally capable in the speed department.

Since they were so competitive with one another, Steve wanted to race Mark first. They had to run several tries before Mark's car came in first by just inches, thus eliminating Steve from competition. Mark's car won first place in the entire event. If Steve hadn't insisted on racing Mark at the outset, we possibly would have had both first and second place winners. I was taking college classes at night at Drury college and unable to attend the competition.

One day Mark went outside to ride his bike, but he couldn't find it anywhere. He thought it was stolen. We lived around the corner from a small grocery store. Sherry had sent Mark to the store for bread. He had bought the bread and walked home, forgetting he had ridden his bike to the store.

Grover and Bonnie (Dad & Mom)

CHAPTER 16

Guns in Our Family

All my children were instructed in the use of guns. When they were younger, they all received BB guns, including daughters and granddaughters, and were taught safety principles. I would place a target on the garage door and a board on the ground ten feet away. No one was allowed to have a gun in hand unless everyone was behind the board. If anyone disobeyed, target practice was over and the guns were all put away until another day. Sometimes cousins or special friends would visit and they all had to abide by the same rules.

On winter days when the weather was too bad for the children to play outside their BB guns were useless unless we figured out how to use them in the house. I had a large 3'x 3'x 4' paper box that I set in the far corner of the living room. I hung a blanket down the middle of the box on a broomstick. The fired BBs would enter the box, hit the curtain, and fall into the box. We had target practice in bad weather without losing a single BB.

Greg McClease, a cousin, was taking target practice one day and his BB gun misfired. He was trying to fix the problem and was looking at the end of the barrel. When he jarred the gun, it fired the BB, hitting him in the forehead. Though it didn't break the skin he assumed he had a BB in his brain and asked his aunt Sherry why he hadn't died yet? Of course, he wasn't actually hurt, but he learned an important Lesson.

As they got older and began to hunt, I gave them each a single shot 20 gauge shot gun, which was appropriate for hunting squirrels and rabbits.

Buying trees and shrubs was not in our budget, though they were needed. A friend trimmed his shrubs and gave me the cuttings from his bushes I dug a hole and planted them using plenty of water and they grew.

As our family numbers grew and we needed a larger house, we moved to the house on Market Street, Mark become our lawn mower and it increased the yard size considerably. I bought a large-back-wheel push mower for Mark and he not only kept our yard mowed but got his first paying lawn mowing job.

As our family grew so did our need for two cars. We acquired a 1939/40 model Plymouth with fluid drive that our children named Old Power Puff. Shifting wasn't necessary unless more power was needed and was the prerogative of the driver. It wasn't necessary for starting from a standing stop. It was a good old car. Normally, I drove the Plymouth to work and Sherry drove our better family car. Occasionally when I was out of town, I took the good car and left Sherry with Old Power Puff. It was ok for dad to drive, but the children didn't want their friends to see them in it. When Sherry would take them to school, they ask her to park a block away and they would walk. They were ashamed of my car. I put a radio in the glove compartment and listened to the news on the way to work. I wish I still had that car.

One day when my family was still at home and the weather was extremely warm, we took a trip to the Dairy Queen in our station wagon. When we arrived, the children began calling out their orders: peanut parfait, banana splits, chocolate sundaes and so on. First of all, I couldn't remember them all. Second, I couldn't have carried all of that, and third, I wasn't sure if I had the funds to pay the bill. So, I got everyone a regular vanilla cone. Back at the car, I was met with much disappointment. My response to all their complaining was, "I gave you a choice, didn't I? At the time they were not happy, but later we all laughed about the choice I had given them.

Once when Shelley was in kindergarten, she and I took my airplane and went flying together. We followed the railroad tracks east out of Kirksville looking for her brothers who were hunting for rabbits. They heard the plane, and thinking I might be the conservation agent, they hid and we couldn't find them. It's illegal to hunt on railroad tracks. I was allowing Shelley to handle the controls of the plane. She was so small she could handle the wheel or the pedals but not both at the same time; she landed the plane with some help. On the drive home she said, "Dad, I'm going to tell my class about this in show and tell tomorrow."

A few days later I said, "Shelley, how did your class go?" She answered "You know I'm the only kid in that class who can fly an airplane."

 I often tried to spend individual time with my children. Shelley and I were in the car and decided on a special day. Calling Sherry and informing her we were leaving town we spent the day at Worlds of Fun in Kansas City. On that trip I let her drive on the I-35 freeway. She performed flawlessly. Shelley did things when she decided it was time, never when it was suggested.

She has always been resolute and determined. She had personalized license plates on her Jeep that read IMSLY (her initials, Shelley Layne Youngblood). She became a registered nurse. Of our six children, Shelley was the most challenging to raise, yet she is an excellent parent. She and her mother were close. She married Shane and became a caring mother to his two beautiful daughters, together, they had two sons and two grandchildren.

Actions say more than words. If friends or neighbors are sick, Shelley is the first to mow their lawn or take them food. Sherry and I had a home with a little more than two acres. Shelley kept it mowed and the flower beds clean and nice looking (she is especially fond of Hosta's). Shelley has retired from a nurse for the Kirksville School and since bottle-feeds calves on her farm in Greentop, Missouri.

99

Early in life Julie developed irritable bowel syndrome and had to be hospitalized. The time and effort needed to care for her caused some of our children to complain that they didn't get the attention they needed. As a parent I tried to avoid such a situation.

Once, not long after new white vinyl siding had been installed on our house, Julie backed out of her parking spot and hit the corner of the house. Distraught, she went up to her room and cried. I went upstairs to comfort her and tried to assure her we could fix it. I also told her when her brothers found out she would probably suffer more ridicule. I gave her twenty dollars and suggested she go shopping.

Later, she partially recovered her health, married, and became a very talented hairdresser. Her marriage didn't last but she has two beautiful daughters and three grandchildren. She still deals with health issues and attends Missouri State University online. She lives in Springfield, Missouri. She plays the piano and writes excellent worship songs, often about the rough times in her life.

She wrote the following song an gave me permission to put it the book. She sang it to me on Father's Day 2020.

When my mom and dad fell in love and married
They started out an adventure that would be
Full of winding roads and eventually six children
Our house was filled with love, we were a happy family

When my dad came home, he would head into the kitchen.
He would hug my mom as she was cooking at the stove
He'd say, "Honey, thank you for giving me this family."
Oh! how he loved her so...
And he'd say,

Honey, do you know how much I love you,

Darlin" Sweetheart, you mean the world to me
I'm so glad you came on this great adventure
How I love you so.... you mean the world to me

When my sister Suz was ready to get married
They didn't have the change to buy a wedding ring
So, my mom slipped her ring off her wedding finger
Oh, how she loved her so...

And she said, Honey do you know how much I love you
Darlin' Sweetheart you mean the world to me
Let this wedding ring be a token of my blessing
How I love you so...Go create your family

There're so many memories I would like to tell
Of good times and bad times and how they served us well
One thing's for certain, this I know for sure
That the love they poured in us, is a love that will endure

There was a time when I was so heartbroken,
The pain so bad that I could barely breathe
My Dad sat down as I was playing the piano
He put his arms around me...as my tears fell on the keys
and he said Honey, do you know how much I love you
Darlin, sweetheart you mean the world to me
If I could take this pain, I would gladly bear it for you
Oh, believe in me...you mean the world to me

There are so many memories I would like to tell
of good times and bad times and how they served us well
One thing for certain, this I know for sure'
That the love they poured in us, is a love that will endure
Cause they said Honey.....

Susie is very intelligent and excellent in school. Our family practice of giving a dollar for each A received on a report card was quickly abandoned when she started school. She was the first of our children to write a song. Susie married Stan, a fellow student at Northeast Missouri State University. Susie and Stan went through hard times when the children were young, divorced, and I had the privilege of reuniting them two years later. Today they are going strong. Their four children have given them five grandchildren. Susie has worked as a teacher, Registered Nurse, college instructor, and currently practices as a Certified Registered Nurse Anesthetist in south Missouri. Stan can be counted on to fix any problems that arise at their house.

Tracy is very unique. As a child she was resolved and determined, but happy. She worked for a season for Sherry in her medical office in Kirksville, Missouri. Later, she branched out on her own and established a transcription business that concentrated on doctors' patient records. In order to operate within the law, she developed a website approved by HIPAA. She sold that business to a group of physicians who saw patients and taught in a medical school. When she and her family moved to Florida, she started a second transcription business, this time for the federal government. She employed several typists who worked from their homes. An economic downturn in VA funding ended that business. She is a master gardener, an accomplished pianist and song writer. She is married to the former chief of police of Kirksville, Missouri. He brought one son into their marriage. She gave birth to two other boys and adopted Ana out of Mexico. They now live in Texas and have four children; three sons, a daughter and six grandchildren.

Once Steve gave me his car keys and took mine. We traded cars because mine looked better. His car had been repaired with a hood we bought at a salvage yard; it was a different color than his car and he wanted to impress a blond-headed girl. When he was delivering papers, he broke the large picture window in Sheryl's parents' house and later he married Sheryl. They have two daughters, one son, and three grandchildren. Steve worked for Walmart before he began pastoring churches. He is currently at Cedar Valley Community Church in Hollister, Missouri which was established by his great grandfathers George and Powell Youngblood.

How to Raise Children
Many decisions that affect our future must be made on the spur of the moment, without the benefit of advice, maturity and experience. They must be made with the information at hand, based on current circumstances and socially accepted norms; the soundness of those decisions can only be measured after the fact, at a future time, and are often made by very young parents. Often the responsibility of raising children come when parents are only teens themselves. Sherry and I were both in our teens when we married and raised two sons and four daughters. None of them were alike. They all had separate characteristic, needs, temperaments, and abilities; We just made the best decision we could at the time, hoping things would turn out.

My Assessment

As I look back to my late sixties and early seventies I was, driving a school bus for the Kirksville School system, teaching troubled youth at the Bruce Normile Juvenile Justice facility and working with autistic children in middle school. Now, just ten or eleven years later it seems like only yesterday. Since I have totally retired, birthdays are coming far too often. Now I spend much of my time praying, writing and just mediating.

I still can do most activities without glasses, although I must admit I can see a little better when I wear them, so when I read, I use them. I don't belong to AARP. That is for old people, and I will never join. I don't need or want any discounts. No cane for me, I don't limp when I walk, It's just maybe a little slower. As I talk daily with the Lord, I'm letting Him know that I don't want to die young.

Reflecting on the past has fallen to me since Sherry recently passed away. Now, I am left to consider the "affects" of decisions we made as we raised our children. I find it's much like looking at the water of a reflection pool: sometimes the picture is a little blurry when a breeze blows across the surface but just wait a minute and it clears again.

Where once I was the chief care giver my roll has changed; my children now are assuming that roll. Now, they have become concerned for my wellbeing. I must not lift anything very heavy or large, no climbing on a ladder past the first rung. They are insisting my housing must be close to at least one of them. They think I am no longer capable of driving my car, so I humor them and just hand over the keys, although when they aren't around, I go and drive anywhere I want.

Often a new belt, a shirt or a new pair of pants appear that are new or sometimes slightly worn, but look almost new.

Susie, Shelley or Tracy has been to the thrift store or a garage sale. A set of knee pads for garden work or prize butter dish with a handle on the lid showed up, Shelley had been to Rutledge dog and gun sale. When my bedside clock malfunctions, another clock appears. Frequent phone calls from Julie just to hear my voice, but actually wanting help with her geology course; she has no idea what topographical maps are.

Mark, who is battling a physical situation that saps his strength, makes a 400-mile round trip to talk with his dad and have lunch. Steve just comes to hang out and often sleeps in the spare bedroom. He makes fun of me when I make him get up and eat the breakfast I have cooked for him. We take frequent drives in the country counting deer and just spending time together.

All hands were on deck when we made the 350 mile move to South Missouri. Jeremy, a grandson, brought youth from the church and made quick work loading the rental truck. My children, including sons-in-law, delivered and unpacked; we were able to resume life as if nothing had happened. When Sherry was hospitalized for the last time the four girls provided 24 hours round the clock coverage. I recently sold my house in Cassville and moved to Aurora, Missouri. And again, my children settled me in my new home which is very comfortable and located next door to Stan and Susie Small.

In my latter years, I now can appraise and evaluate the results of decisions Sherry and I made years ago, when our children were young and still at home; they seem to have turned out ok.

Also, you who are reading this and know our children can judge together with me the kind of job we done.

How do you raise children? The Bible gives us some vital instructions:

We are called sheep, and sheep produce young sheep; under the direction of the shepherd these little lambs are cared for as part of the flock. Palms 23 gives us some good instruction for raising our children - as you read it look for the following needs of a sheep that is under your care.

Four needs of a sheep:

    1. Provision,

    2. A leader,

    3. Protection and

    4. A Calm dwelling place.

Provide these four things then leave it up to God!

A Major Tragedy

In 2020 Steven a 30-year-old grandson belonging to Steve and Sheryl was found dead of unknown circumstances. He left a wife, Kayla and son Jeffery. I was looking through my files and am including my answer to a letter he had sent informing me that he had joined the Missouri National guard.

Dear Steven

Your dad gave us your letter today, we read it on the way to Columbia, it was very good to hear from you. How well do I remember basic training! The YES SIRS AND NO SIRS, ending every sentence with Sir. I remember the burr haircuts, the standing at attention and of course the calisthenics. If you were overweight, you lost weight and if you were under weight, you gained. After a while, I became so hungry, I didn't care what the mess hall served I ate it, as much and as fast as I could. Although I really liked SOS. (S...t on a shingle) I went from 130# to 150#. I kind-a wish I could do the opposite now.

I really didn't miss the getting up at 4:30 A.M. for reveille and hearing the flight commander say all present and accounted for Sir. Everywhere we went, we marched in formation. I liked to march, it sounded like one giant boot hitting the ground at once. I remember putting tape on the coins for the washing machine. The coin would trip the machine, and then be retrieved for the next wash.

We learned about midnight requisitions. We would borrow a buffer (always after dark) and return it just before the sun came up. We always had a clean shiny floor ready for inspection the next morning. I liked to be the pusher on K P. It was always possible to steal food for an evening snack. I hated doing the grease pit and peeling potatoes. I didn't mind the butcher shop; it was always cool and we usually just handled the meat after the real butchers cut it into pieces.

I am glad for the experience but wouldn't want to do it again...As you probably know I went from basic at Parks AFB in San Francisco (I was in the Air Force) to Cheyenne, Wyoming for training communication machines. Next to Scott AFB in Illinois near St Louis for cryptographic machine repair training and finally to the pentagon where I worked in Headquarters Communications Squadron.

I was disappointed with the attitude of many of my fellow airmen. They were lazy, felt like they had it made and did little to better themselves, but just wanted the next promotion and the bigger check. They didn't have the will or capability of making a living on the outside in the competitive world. I never gave any serious consideration to stay in for multiple tours. I applied for flying status but the alphabet was against me, by the time they got to the Y's all the positions were filled

I am very proud of you. This can be an awesome experience. It sounds like you are putting your all into what you are doing. I know you are excelling, so just keep it up. This is the way of life; you get out what you put into it. I don't know about coming to the graduation but we'll see what happens,

Grandma and I are praying for you. We both know that God will lead you in his will for your life. You got a rocky start but have done all you can to make things right and that is very important. If I don't make it to your graduation, I will sure see you when you get home.

Just for your information, tonight Grandma and I were sitting in the living room and saw two large deer both does and a smaller deer just across the road by our mail box.

May God bless you and we'll be seeing you soon
Grandpa and Grandma

 Mark began working at Mansfield IGA grocery and eventually married the boss's daughter. Barbara had two young daughters that easily fit in and became a part of our family. The daughters have now married and Mark and Barb now have eight grandchildren. Later, after he and Barbara were married the grocery store closed, and he worked for the Kirksville Police department achieving the rank of Sergeant. Then he resigned and pursued a college education. He now has a master's degree from Columbia University in Columbia, Missouri. He is truly the big brother and was very protective of his sisters as they grew up.

When the eclipse of the sun occurred (Aug 21, 2017), he drove four hours down to Aurora and took me to his home in Columbia, which was a better vantage point. He also had Shelley drive down from Greentop and the three of us had a cold cut lunch and watched the eclipse from the balcony of his apartment. They call themselves, "the book ends," since he is the oldest and Shelley is the youngest. He then returned me to my home. He drove a total of sixteen hours so that I could see the eclipse better.

In our household with seven teenagers and nine vehicles, calls such as the following were not uncommon.

"Dad, I have a red light on the dash of my car is that important?"

"Dad, I left the door slightly open and now my car won't start. Can you help?"

"Dad, I'm at Walmart and I locked the keys in my car, what should I do?" were questions I often received by phone.

Slowly, the boys began leaving home, but they still called when their cars wouldn't start, especially in cold weather.

I bought Julie an older car because of her illness and inability to work. One time she was at Thousand Hills Lake near Kirkville and a tire went flat. She drove the car home ruining the tire. When I asked her about it, she said, "I drove slowly and thought it would be ok."

Susie had an older car I don't remember its make. I do remember it was light green. She told me on a trip up to Iowa to see Stan her car developed a strange noise. When I asked her what she did to check on the noise, she said she just rolled up the window.

The remains of the Youngblood Service Station and grocery store.

Pine Top Church
Mother pastored this church for a season.

CHAPTER 17

Faith in The Ozarks

Brother Deward Watson usually set up a tent in a vacant field just south of the Youngblood Store and conducted revival meetings every year. Loud speakers on top of his car broke the afternoon calm as he drove his car along the highway telling folks the meeting would start Saturday night at seven o clock.

"Bring your guitars and any other instruments and come to church ready to sing praises and hear the word of God," he would say. And the tent would be full every night.

There were some folding chairs but mostly chunks of wood cut from trees with boards to sit on. The altars were constructed somewhat like the seats but lower to the ground and located up front for the people to come and pray. Someone would bring a load of sawdust to keep down the dust. Extension cords, stretching from our station, powered lights hanging from the tent poles. These meetings usually lasted two to three weeks. Many people were changed as they surrendered their lives to the Lord. I would go out under the tent during the day when there was no church service and I would find Prince Albert tobacco cans, half full of tobacco, under the altar where people had prayed and laid down their habits as they turned their lives over to the Lord.

I saw my Uncle Clarence stand, repent, and make restitution to another brother in the congregation. A neighbor in the community had hired him to take a load of hogs to the market in Springfield. The hogs had brought a few more cents per pound than was expected. He received his hauling fee and kept the extra money from the sale of the hogs. He gave the extra money to the man there in the meeting. I watched his life for years; Uncle Clarence had the real thing.

In 1959/60 Sherry and I began attending Cedar Valley Pentecostal Church when we returned to Missouri. This church had its beginning from a revival meeting conducted in an old-school building by my Grandfather George Youngblood in the early 1900s. The old building was moved to higher ground and located a few miles north of the Arkansas State Line on US highway 65. The name came from its original location now covered by the waters of Table Rock Dam. My mother had taken Sherry to a revival meeting conducted by a student from S of O (School of the Ozarks - now called College of the Ozarks). We became committed Christians and have both served God the balance of our lives.

Most of its members were our longtime friends and family and all gave top priority to prayer. My decision to turn my life over to the Lord was the result of her recommitting her life to the Lord.

God had been dealing with me for several years and I knew then was the time to become a Christian, and so I did.

Sunday afternoon, before the night service, found us at various houses praying. On weekends and especially Sundays we lived in the very presence of God. It was not unusual for several couples to make the drive to Springfield for Bible study with Sherry and me. My job in Springfield with Southwestern Bell Telephone Company made the fifty-mile one-way drive to church difficult. We could not attend mid-week services or many special church services.

After about a year I reluctantly moved our family to a small church near where we lived called The Full Gospel Pentecostal

Church on the corner of Hovey and Nettleton. Our pastor Oneida Robertson also taught that prayer was the most important activity one could pursue. Her husband Bill built a small house in their back yard and she would spend hours in that house in prayer. Her life was exemplary of a Christian who prayed. I have seen her preach when the power of God would come on her and she would fall out under His power behind the pulpit. After a while the service would be dismissed, and we would finally leave and return home with her still under the power of God.

Next in importance to the life of prayer is a lifestyle of holiness! We adopted the lifestyle of our friends in the church. That style of living expressed what we thought at the time was holiness. We were taught that our commitment to God was shown by our lifestyle, including our appearance.

The women didn't cut their hair, put on makeup, or wear shorts. They had to be properly covered. They wore only dresses, no pants. According to scripture they could not wear anything that pertained to what a man would wear. My shirts were all long sleeves and I never consumed tobacco or alcoholic products. Our jewelry was limited to our wedding rings that represented our covenant with one another before God. We didn't attend any movies, listen to secular songs, watch television, or attend any questionable places of amusement. As our family grew in number so did our understanding of our commitment to God.

A study of the Old Testament reveals when a King needed to know the will of God, he would call for a prophet. When the king personally humbled himself, he would remove his royal robes and dress in apparel made from cloth used to make sacks for transporting goods on the back of a mule. He would then put ashes on the sackcloth and humble his heart. These actions represented his recognition that only God can help. He often received the deliverance he desired for himself and his people.

One time when the church announced a special scheduled time of prayer, I took a gunny sack (burlap sack) and some ashes from

113

the burn barrel and went to church. We had hard wood floors. I spread out the sack, put ashes on it, and got on my face before God. The presence of God came on me and I lost track of time. I literally was groaning in the Spirit. It seemed only minutes, but more than an hour had gone by. When I came to myself, I was praying for my father who I later learned had just had a heart attack. This happened in the 60's when we didn't have the medical understanding we have now. My dad recovered and lived seventeen more years, giving his life to the Lord before he died in 1979.

His presence that came upon me at the time seemed to be described in

Romans 8:26 (NLT) *26 And the Holy Spirit helps us in our weakness. For example, we don't know what God wants us to pray for. But the Holy Spirit prays for us with groanings that cannot be expressed in words.*

Our little church body never grew much in numbers but the effect on this Youngblood family has never weakened. We still recognize the importance of the manifest presence of God and its effect on the life of an individual. We now realize that true holiness is not necessarily how we dress but is a Godly attribute that is in/and comes from the heart. We must dress in an acceptable and decent manner. Our apparel must not be provocative but in a manner that honors God.

We also know that prayer is no less important but it must come from the heart, in the Spirit, and specifically for the plan of God to be accomplished.

When I went into management for the telephone company, I gave it my all. I left the house before the children were awake and returned after they were in bed. They would ask their mother, "Is dad in town?"

I told myself I wanted to achieve this or that, make this much money so we could do this or that. Special time with my family was a future goal. My pastor took me aside and told me I had my priorities wrong; that I was seriously neglecting my family. During my time of inner-searching God spoke to me saying, "It's not the destination that is important but the journey. Pay more attention to life with your loved ones now, don't wait until some future happening."

I again lost track of my priorities when pastoring the church in Kirksville, Missouri. Having a television and radio ministry along with my pastoral duties again found me going ninety miles per hour. One day Susie came to me and said dad, "Could I make an appointment to see you in the next few days?"

Those words were like a knife in my stomach "Honey," I said, "Why do you think you need an appointment to see your father?"
"Dad you are so busy I didn't want to bother you," she said.

I immediately called my girls together and repented for becoming too involved and neglecting my family. I set aside a special night each week for each daughter to have a date with their father—the boys had left home by that point. We went to the restaurant they chose and shopping after our dinner. I made a rule, even if I was preaching and a phone call came in from any of my family, I was to be interrupted. I would finish my sermon later. My family knew they were first.

Through our marriage, I watched Sherry, the teenage bride, change into an accomplished individual. She became an excellent wife, mother and homemaker. She mastered the ability of caring for a large family with no one, including her husband, ever feeling neglected. She later managed a major medical office with ten providers and thirty-five employees. She was an excellent role model. She was instrumental in seeing her husband, our children, and both her parents turn wholeheartedly to God. Our children all love the Lord and have instilled in their children love and respect for God.

Proverbs 31:28 (NKJV) 28 Her children rise up and call her blessed; Her husband *also,* and he praises her: *(This has and is Happening-God is so good)*

Preaching in Mombasa Kenya

CHAPTER 18

My Bird Dog

I bought my first dog, a black and white long-haired dog with a reputation for being a good quail dog and he turned out to be a pretty good dog. I don't remember his name but he would hunt close to us and would find quail. He would hold the point until we flushed the covey and often would find and retrieve the downed bird. We usually came home with our limit.

The dog had one problem, which is probably how I got him so cheap. If we ran across a rabbit that dog would chase it and he was gone. We had to stop hunting until we could get him back and settled down.

I inquired around about what I should do to break him from

running rabbits. I got a lot of advice. I tried everything. I shot a rabbit and tied it around his neck and he wore it all day. Another fellow told me to aim high and shoot in the direction of the dog and sting him with a few of the pellets from the outer lower pattern of shot. The next time we went hunting, true to form, that dog began to run a rabbit. I aimed high

117

and fired, I just didn't aim high enough.

Misty Red was a registered Brittany Spaniel that I bought as a young dog intending to have her trained to point and retrieve quail. The fellow I bought her from guaranteed she wouldn't get pregnant which was a requirement as I wanted to hunt her in the upcoming season. I built a good pen next to a little outbuilding where she could go in cold weather or rain. The children loved her and gave her much attention. Too much I thought. I was told children playing with her could be detrimental to training her to hunt. The children won; I just couldn't tell them to leave her alone.

Sherry worked at the Meadow Gold Dairy as a secretary; the office was two blocks from our house and she often walked to work. She got an urgent call to come home. The children had been playing with the dog and she began having pups. There were eight little pups scattered over the backyard when Sherry got here. That guy I had bought the dog from was right she wouldn't get pregnant, she already was. Needless to say, she didn't hunt that year. Later she was stolen. I never got to train or hunt her.

Sour Dough was my pride and joy. He was a beagle, loud and slow, perfect for hunting rabbits. I gave Mr. Jefferies twenty-five dollars for him. I could let him loose in an area where rabbits were, and stand still. He was too slow to catch a rabbit, but his voice was loud. When he struck a rabbit trail he would begin to bark, which would cause the rabbits to start moving. I would wait and here would come the rabbit usually toward me. Sour Dough helped put lots of meat on our table.

Sherry would put those cleaned cut up rabbits in a large pan and slowly cook them until they became tender and the broth made lots of gravy. Man!!, with a hot biscuit, I'm getting hungry just thinking about it.

We lived in town so Sour Dough couldn't be turned loose to run free. I had an overhead wire that ran from the front corner of my garage to a large tree. I could hook his chain to that wire and he could move a long way. It was better than tying him. He had a warm dog house, an automatic dog food feeder that would hold a twenty-five-pound sack of dog food, and an electric bucket to keep the water from freezing in winter. He had everything he needed.

I went out to give him some fresh water one day and he looked so pitiful being tied up that I turned him loose to run for a while. He was limping when he came back. The vet thought he must have been hit by a car. One of his rear hips was broken. The vet put a cast on him. He could get around pretty good with that cast so I tied him back on his overhead wire. But the weather turned cold and I didn't have the heart to leave him outside in the cold. I brought him into the back room of the house.

That dog ate Sherry's couch right down to the springs in the cushions. Man was I in trouble. I didn't like to spend money on a dog in the first place. I usually bought medicine for rabies, worms, and distemper at the farm store and administered it myself. I had spent all that money on a vet and then I had to buy a new couch. Having rabbit for supper was getting way too expensive. Just as soon as I got him completely well, the vet took off the cast and I gave him away.

In addition to dogs, our house was a menagerie. We had tropical fish, hamsters, gerbils, guinea pigs, cats, mice, rats, snakes, hermit crabs, insects and worms; you name it at one time or another we had them. One-time Sherry opened the refrigerator and there neatly on a plate were several worms. Shelley said they were hot so she was cooling them off.

Once, Rick (my brother who lived with us for a time) brought home an alligator. We found it in the bath tub. Shelley had a parrot that bit her and she got rid of it.

Another time, Tracy woke her mother with a small garter snake wrapped around her arm, holding its head between her thumb and finger. Sherry opened her eyes with that snake in her face. She became wide awake rather quickly and for an instant Tracy's life was in danger. Tracy just wanted permission to keep it as a pet.

Tracy was my dark-haired hazel-eyed determined child. She had already decided when she came to me with her petitions.

119

"Dad. I want a monkey, if you will get me a monkey, I won't ask for another thing the rest of my life. I want a monkey more than anything in my life. I will take care of it and you won't have to do a thing."

Obviously, she didn't get a monkey and we laughed about it later, but I will always remember the resolve and determination she exhibited at that young age; which, by the way, hasn't diminished, but has become more intense.

While there was no monkey, she has had almost everything else. Her room became a maze of small animal houses, tunnels, exercise wheels for rats, mice, hamsters, gerbils and guinea pigs. These plastic animal tunnels circumvented the entire room. Some adjustments were required because she soon learned that often several gerbils together in the same cage eat their young and must be separated soon after birth.

Otherwise, she kept her room clean and the animals fed with no problems until Susie's cat came on the scene. Susie's resolve was a little more practical. She had to have a cat, not a tropical animal. Sherry and I had never allowed an animal to have free run of the inside of our house. We made an exception for the cat, exacting a promise from Susie of excellent care and cleanliness. And I must admit things went along fine for a few weeks, but that changed when we heard a blood-curdling scream from Tracy's room. There on the floor was a half-eaten hamster. The door to her room had been left open and the cat had fresh meat for a meal.

Another problem presented itself; we thought the cat was using the litter box, but soon after the hamster incident we began to notice a faint smell in the living room. We pulled the couch away from the wall and discovered the source of the odor. The cat had used "behind the couch" area, not the litter box. Susie was given a roll of paper towels, a pan of warm sudsy water and a rag. When she had finished, the room smelled very good but her desire for a cat had waned. The cat became a barn cat out in the country. Our household went back to normal, if you can call us normal.

120

I was the initiator of our tropical fish collection that consisted of bubble nest builders, egg layers, and a live bearer. As the small fry would show up in our aquarium, I would force boiled egg yolk through a cheese cloth and introduce a fine powder for the young to eat. We had fish aquariums at multiple locations in the house. The aquarium in the family room contained five hundred gallons of water and sat on cinder blocks. Other aquariums contained several species of fresh water tropical fish: guppies, sword tails, neon, zebras, gourami, mollies, black molly angel fish, Plecostomus, tetra, and tiger barbs. Some were fed brine shrimp, others just plain fish food. Occasionally I would come across mosquito larva in standing water. I called them wiggle tails and the fish really liked them. Uncle Albert, Rick's piranha ate hamburger meat and small gold fish.

Another dog I loved was Moose. He came from Shelley after she was married, the phone call was like this.

"Dad, I really messed up today," she said on the phone.

"Honey," I asked "what do you mean, you really messed up?"

"I saw a dog on the local TV station's dog pound program, went out there to see it and I brought him home."

"What kind of dog is it"? I asked.

"A miniature Doberman Pinscher and his name is Moose," she said. The vision of a tiny Doberman Pinscher with the name "Moose" made me smile.

Moose had not had a good life. He was about seven and had been abused, and mistreated. He was found locked in a room abandoned by his former owner. He was treated medically for a cut on his neck. After he came to live with Shane and Shelley, he was not returning to health. Dr. Moore diagnosed heart worms with no chance of recovery due to his rundown condition. The treatment was expensive but they began it immediately. He had to have a special diet and needed to be kept quiet as possible (no barking) to keep pressure off the heart. Moose survived and regained much of his health.

Moose and I become friends. He greeted me very warmly and became my dog while I was in Shane and Shelley's home. He attended baseball games hidden in a large purse Shelley would carry on her shoulder. (Usually, animals were not allowed at sporting events) Occasionally he would come home with me. He could always tell as we turned toward my house. When Shane and Shelley were on a trip Moose stayed with Sherry and me. At breakfast time I got my eggs and Moose got his egg served on a real plate. He would not eat off a paper plate.

We had a special relationship until the last two years. Milky white cataracts caused blindness, he could no longer get up or down from a chair, and picking him up sometime caused pain. When his eyes became worse and he was in constant pain, he had to be put down. That was a tough decision. Moose lived fourteen years, in doggie years that is age 98.

Realizing the time was near I glanced at my watch and knew when Moose's life ended. I was traveling from Cassville, Missouri to Springfield, Mo. and felt very sad. He went to sleep with no pain and never woke up.

I know that a dog is not a person, and not nearly as important as my children and grandchildren, but Moose brought out a tenderness and compassion that I would have never experienced. I felt terrible losing my friend but decided, it's better to have had a friend and lose him then never having had a friend.

CHAPTER 19

Leaving Southwest Bell Telephone Company

When I was thirty-seven, I resigned my position with SWBT, for family reasons. My two sons came to me one day and asked me if our family would be changing locations and moving to another city or town with the telephone company. I said, "I'm sure we will, we could go back to Springfield, or St Louis and maybe even Kansas City". They said, "Dad we love it here in Kirksville, can we just stay here? We don't want to leave our friends; we just don't want to leave."

Shortly after that conversation I took a position with Delbert Hawkins, a close friend and owner of Hawkins insurance agency who had approached me earlier asking me to consider working for him. Immediately I began managing a weekly paper called the Kirksville Area Shopper. He had just bought this local weekly shopper. I became editor (or actually chief cook and bottle washer). My responsibilities as editor were selling advertising, designing the ads, collecting payments, preparation of copy for printing, taking the copy to printer and mailing ten thousand pieces each week at the post office. The business was gaining notoriety and acceptance as more advertisers were seeing results. As we gained advertisers our cash flow increased and there was less and less white on the pages. The business was gaining strength when a strike in the timber industry caused a shortage of paper products. The local newspaper that was printing our paper needed the paper for their personal production and could no longer service us, we had no choice, we had to close down our operation.

123

The positive side of their venture is, I had received an education about an industry that hadn't been on my bucket list.

I had taken the necessary training and became licensed in Missouri as an all-class insurance broker and real-estate broker. I sold life, accident and health insurance and was successful as an estate planner. During this time, I managed a savings and loan office, established a casualty insurance agency—later selling it for a profit.

My real-estate sales didn't materialize until a few years later when I moved to Huston, Texas, that story is later in a second book.

At one point in this period, everything closed in around me. A banker friend asked if I would assume the loan on a few mobile homes and rent them. He said he would add additional cash for upgrades and repair and give me a favorable interest rate. After consideration I felt it was a venture with promise and said, "yes".

The endeavor fared well for a while. As additional units were added expenses grew. Frozen pipes, vacancies, failed water heaters and other appliances, as well as fixed expenses ate up my business cash account. The time I used to manage the rental units reduced the time I had for insurance calls and my sales dropped which resulted in a dire lack of money for our general household needs.

One day a bill came due and I had no money. I skipped a mortgage payment to buy food. I continued the juggling act, hoping things would turn around, until the utility company disconnected my household natural gas. My house payments were several months in arrears and my income was almost nil. Then came the dreaded eviction notice: all payments due or we sell your house on the courthouse steps. I pictured our family on the curb. I had failed as a business man, a father, and a husband.

Thinking time would cure the problem, I went to the banker to discuss my business affairs. Surprisingly, he was looking for an investment. He offered to take my rental business, assume my debt, and run it as his private side business. My answer was yes!

Now I turned to the problems of finding sufficient funds to pay my accumulated back debts and to keep our household afloat. It was winter time, Sherry and I with the four girls still at home began living in two downstairs rooms heated with electric room heaters. These rooms were partitioned off using blankets. We still had electricity; water heated on the electric range was poured into the bath tub to bathe the children. Our food was supplied using small residual checks from my past insurance sales. Sometimes our return home from church services was interrupted when our car ran out of gasoline and we just walked the rest of the way. We just parked the car and walked home. The next day I would drain the lawn mower and use for gas to bring the car home. My friends didn't know we were having these problems.

There was no other place to look but God. I began to pray, often on the living room floor, for most of the night. Julie's health deteriorated during this time. A trip to the bathroom wore her out so much that she had to rest for several hours before she had enough strength to do it again. The school sent a teacher to help her keep up with her studies.

Part of my prayer life was to lie across the bed and pray in tongues. One day I asked God to tell me what I was saying as I prayed. The Holy Spirit revealed that I was praying for Julie to stop worrying about an algebra test. Evidently, the Spirit of God is concerned about our every problem.

One day without knowing how or what to pray I was walking the streets, quoting every scripture verse I could think of, "Jesus wept", "For God so loved the world." Finally, "The Lord is my shepherd I shall not want."

The Spirit stopped me and said, "What did you just say?"

"I shall not want," I said.

"Do you want?" He asked.

"You know that I do," I said.

He said, "Say on."

"He makes me lie down in green pastures," I said.

125

He asked me what that meant and I said, "It means there is so much grass, their bellies are full and they are laying down in the abundance."

"Okay, say on," He said.

"He leads me by the still waters."

"What does that mean?" He asked.

"Still waters mean deep, more water than enough," I said.

"Am I your shepherd?" He asked.

At that moment I realized I was living my life according to my will and purpose; I immediately repented and asked Him to be my shepherd. My pain, stress, and dread of facing the day lifted and hope took its place. It is so refreshing to have the God of the Universe speak directly to you. I didn't know what was going to happen but I felt a peace I hadn't known for a while.

A few days later I visited my parents in Ridgedale, and my father gave me a $1,500.00 check as payment for a bathroom I had installed in their house several months earlier. I had intended it as a gift, but he hadn't considered it a gift. He had saved up money to repay what he considered a debt. All at once my house payment and past-due utility bills were caught up, and I no longer had a group of rentals. I had a new start.

A Friend Needed Help

A few months later an opportunity to help and bless someone came when a special friend was looking for a fresh start for his family. I worked in the health insurance market and he thought maybe this could be the new beginning for his family. My family of eight enlarged to thirteen when He and his wife and their three small girls came to live with us. I began training the two of them in health insurance sales. This was an unusual time when we were blessed to have their family join us for this new adventure.

Usually when training a new recruit, the income was split, but their financial need was so great I gave them all of it. After considering this avenue as the opportunity my friends had discovered their answer

126

to their question and returned to Oklahoma with a different outlook on life. We actually had a ball; we are all still friends.

I left the insurance community in 1979, the year my dad died, becoming pastor of First Assembly of God Church in Unionville, Missouri. Sherry and I moved our family (now just four girls at home) to Unionville, Missouri. Just eight months after I had become pastor of the church, I received a call and returned as pastor of Faith Assembly of God in Kirksville, Missouri. Steve, my second son, who is also a minister, became the pastor in Unionville.

A few months into my time at Faith Assembly, God gave me revelation of how he would build his church (Ephesians 4:8-16). Because of the current style of denominational government, I couldn't fully follow the vision I had received from the Lord, so I chose to resign as a denominational minister.

It was 1983 when I resigned my denominational affiliation and began a church called Covenant Life Fellowship (CLF) in a rented space at the Thompson Center at the AT Still Osteopathic School of Medicine using their gymnasium.

This group of believers grew and prospered in number and we became loosely connected with an apostolic team from England. In 1985 at the age of forty-nine I left CLF church with young leaders and ministers which included my sons Steve and Mark and moved to Houston, Texas joining a minister from Sweden who worked as a missionary in Pakistan and Afghanistan. The missionary plans didn't materialize as originally planned. I entered the real-estate market in Texas, in sales, with Century 21 Gold Country and instructor with Champion School of Real Estate teaching candidates who were testing for a real-estate sales license in Texas. Sherry began working for the Fire department in Conroe, Texas.

From time to time, I had traveled back to Kirksville and assisted the church when they were establishing a permanent location in an existing vacant super market building.

In mid-1989 Sherry and I returned to Kirksville; we still owned our home which was leased so we moved into rental facilities. I began working as a business manager in a General Motors Automobile Sales store.

Later that year Sherry received a call from her mother who lived in Branson, Missouri, with disturbing news. A chest x-ray taken when her father was prepping for cataract surgery revealed a large malignant mass in his lung. Earl, in his late eighties, decided against any invasive treatment. They need help.

Sherry and I moved south to Hollister, Missouri to assist Alba, Sherry's sister, with this terrible time. We made our home in a small two-bedroom condo on Lake Taneycomo in Hollister. This location gave Sherry unfettered access to her parents.

Later, as Earl's health began to fail, Sherry moved in with her parents and provided 24/7 coverage. After almost a year of fighting this fatal disease, during one of their many conversations, she had prayed with her dad and he had a personal encounter with the Lord. Earl lost the battle. He died in August, 1991. Growing up, Sherry had been a daddy's girl and at the end of his life they were able to spend many weeks together.

When we returned to Kirksville, I again began in auto sales as business manager in the General Motors Automobile store when I was approached by Jerry McMain asking me to join him in his store as a furniture salesman. I accepted and soon after I opened and managed a furniture store in the vacant Old Montgomery Ward building in Ottumwa, Iowa. I had phenomenal success and in 30 months I was able to turn the store over to him with $150,000 inventory all paid for. The call of God was still strong, I resigned as manager of Tarkim Furniture Store in Ottumwa, Iowa and returned to the church.

After rejoining CLF church staff, a Bible school was in its infancy and growing, I helped negotiate the purchase of a sixty-six room, fully operational hotel to house the college students and became temporary hotel manager. The second floor was rented to the public. A book store, open to the public, provided text books for college class.

Necessary changes included closing current operating bars and making it a smoke free facility. The existing restaurant was staffed by bible school students who needed jobs to pay tuition. We cultivated the banquet business, had some dinner theaters, and promoted the facilities for pastoral conferences. A service club began meeting in our ball room one day a week.

Sherry and I traveled to Berlin, Ohio and met with Jim and Robin Schrock who knew more about hotels and restaurants than we did. They agreed to move to Kirksville, Missouri and take my place. Jim assumed responsibility for the restaurant operation and Robin managed the bookstore/gift shop, located in the hotel. I could now just teach in the Bible school.

The Covenant Life Fellowship Church began to fellowship with a para-church organization called Heartland, located in Ewing, Missouri about forty-five minutes east of Kirksville.

The Travelers hotel, the Bible college, the book store, print shop, web master, and the scheduled conferences became too much for the church to oversee. Steve, the key to the operation was burned out. Several of the staff were traveling to many of the churches that were coming to the conferences.

I was teaching full time in the Bible school, and establishing a church in Plymouth, Massachusetts. For two years, every week on Saturday I traveled from Kansas City International to Boston Logan and returning on Sunday evening for Monday morning classes, approximately two hundred support staff moved to Heartland. I moved with the Bible college. The Heartland group had an excellent policy of receiving anyone in trouble, providing housing, employment, and spiritual help until they could get their lives back in order. One unfortunate result of this move was that the dynamics of the Bible school changed. The original purpose of the Bible college was training young people for parenthood and marriage with the intent of sending them back to their churches as workers.

When troubled youths with drug problems were introduced into the classes everything changed. I'm not against helping anyone in trouble but we should have had separate classes where the requirement and expectations were different. I stayed and taught in Bible School for four semesters and resigned.

Glen Berry is a dear minister friend, who at the time, lived in Tucson, Arizona. We often ministered and traveled together preaching in churches in Chihuahua, Ayutla, Juarez, and Mexico City, Mexico. He, on occasion, would travel with me to the Boston area and speak to the church out there.

I accompanied Mike Lakes; a very dear man that pastored in the four-square organization, to Mombasa, Kenya where I preached several times a day for a week in a local conference. I went on safari, and first hand up close, saw many of the species of animals in the wild.

With the local bishop I visited some remote villages. I met a pastor whose congregation was meeting under a tree out in the bush. I had multiple invites actually, please, please, come back and come to my church was the appeal.

Seeing a need for a traveling Bible school I was making plans for a second trip to Africa where I planned to speak to several pastors in Tanzania, Uganda and Kenya. I expected to take two trips per year and teach two months each trip. Before I could prepare the materials and staff needed to train the nationals in Africa a local need arose. I began teaching troubled young people and working for Kirksville R3 School district as a substitute teacher. I was a teacher full time, math and science in a juvenile justice facility where young people are incarcerated when in trouble with the law. A part of my day was teaching in the lock-down unit. The balance of my day was teaching in the residential unit where kids are housed until the state can find a place for them to go, such as a foster home or in some cases be returned back into their home.

CHAPTER 20

Caring for Our Parents

While in the home of Sherry's parents, she became aware that her mother, suffering from glaucoma; had lost most of her eyesight. Lorene knew her house well enough that no one visiting for a short time could tell she couldn't see. This disease had taken most of her peripheral vision. Her sight was limited to how one could see if they were looking through the barrel of a shot gun.

One day while she was cooking, when Sherry was there, a cloth caught fire and Lorene couldn't see it. Sherry quickly put it out.

Lorene, because of failing eye sight, would use a flash light to find items in the refrigerator but was not able to recognize food that was discolored and/or spoiled. I changed out the 20-watt bulb in her refrigerator to a 200-watt bulb and installed a light fixture of four 36" fluorescent bulbs in the ceiling that provided ample light for the twelve-by-twelve kitchen/eating area. To this day I can still see the light in Lorene's eyes and the joy of a new found freedom to actually be able to see in her kitchen and inside her refrigerator.

Sherry told me that her mother, who, after seeing the effort needed to care for Earl in his later years, said, "Who is going to take care of me?" Seeing my over-eighty-year-old mother-in-law this late in life with no hope in her future struck a chord in my heart.

The lifestyle of Sherry's parents was much different than ours. I allowed no tobacco, alcohol or gambling activities in my home

131

and all three were normal in theirs. A few days later I sat with Lorene at her dining room table and told her she was a major part of my family and would always have a home with us. I told her that I wanted her, now that Earl was gone, to come and live with us and that she would not have to change her life style. I would make sure there was beer in the refrigerator and whatever else she needed or wanted.

Sherry and I returned to Kirksville. Lorene was determined she could live alone, and did for approximately a year. The day she fell and crawled to the phone to get help changed her mind. She came to live with us in the latter part of 1992. She became an extremely important part of our family; we lived together for seven years until her passing in 1999. Her arrival at our house brought changes in our families that were priceless.

My children and grandchildren had unlimited access to their grandmother and great grandmother. Sherry and her mother spent hours together. Her attitude was such a blessing; she was so easy to be around. At times she was reluctant to join us in family activities because she was careful not to get in the way of Sherry and my time together. At first it was difficult for me to buy beer at the grocery store; Sherry did most of the buying. I am just so glad that she didn't smoke or chew tobacco.

Her personal care was minimal; Sherry administered the daily drops for her eyes trying to preserve the shotgun-barrel sight she still had. She stayed alone most week days with a life alert signal available, which was never used. Wanting to do what she could around the house she assumed the duties of folding the clean clothes. Due to her failing eyesight, I have gone to work a few times with one sock red and the other one green. I bought twelve pair of identical black socks and retired all the others. She laughed hard when she saw what I had done.

Not being able to see, she allowed a pot of beans to get too dry, and when they were served for supper little flakes from the pan were mixed in. The beans were a little bitter but we ate them with no complaint. Again, after supper she had a good laugh about how we had treated the meal she had fixed for us. She was a joy to be around. We all laughed often.

One-time her daughter Alba and her husband Donnie came up to celebrate one of Lorene's birthdays. We watched little naked Gunner in the back yard trying to climb up into the water in the bird bath. He was small and still in diapers and we all had a good laugh.

All my daughters would take her shopping and other outings during the week. She taught them how to play the lottery. One scratch ticket yielded a whopping seven dollars. She taught them how to play poker and other card games.

When Seth was very small, she had an open beer can sitting on the floor by her chair. Seth picked it up and tried to drink it but he sputtered and put it back down. After that I would make a joke when others were around, saying playfully "Lorene has lived with us only six months and she has my grandchildren gambling, playing cards, and drinking beer.

Around the house she would often wear a pair of shorts that were much too big. I would kid her about the shorts, saying that she had to take three steps before the shorts would begin to move. I often would come home and say to Sherry and Lorene, "Ok, get in the car, let's go."

"Go where?" Lorene would ask.

"Just get in the car, let's go," I would say.

"You and Sherry go ahead you need to spend time together," she would often say.

"No we all are going," I would tell her.

"I'm not going looking like this!" she would say.

"Yes you are," I would say. "Come on, get in the car."

"Well, I'm going to get my shoes, I'm not going barefoot."

We would usually go south to the small town of Atlanta, Missouri and then west to a farm that maintained a herd of elk. She always enjoyed looking at their large rack of horns. Then I would take another road south down to Macon where we would eat a buffet meal at the Long Branch Restaurant. It was always a good evening.

133

I would usually concoct an account of our outing. I would only tell the made-up story when several people who loved Lorene were around to hear it. I would embellish how embarrassed I was with a woman who would go out in public wearing such outlandish clothing. Of course, I was making fun of the shorts. I would tell how I would stall, find something to do so I wouldn't have to walk into a public place with her wearing those shorts. I would tell how I would enter alone and quietly join them at their table. She would just shake her head as I embellished the story to make her seem visibly out of place wearing those shorts and dressed as she was. She didn't care. The next evening when I came home, she was wearing those shorts.

She always enjoyed our numerous drives around the country side; she especially enjoyed seeing the deer when we went out to Thousand Hills Park. On one outing at the lake when we parked looking out over the water, she commented the water was so calm, not a ripple could be seen. What she couldn't see was that the lake was frozen. We all had a big laugh over the calm looking water.

A major ice storm left us without electricity for a few days. Our light was a kerosene lamp; our heat was a propane tank, normally used in our deer stand, and we cooked our meals on a charcoal grill. We had lots of company. The weather wasn't extremely cold. It was an adventure and she said it was just like old times.

All the grandchildren and many of the great grandchildren spent time with Grandma. She and Julie would write songs and sing them to us. I remember one song they just couldn't get the lyrics to come out right and Lorene said "Use 'the back roads of my mind.'" It fit perfectly.

It was always a very special time when Alba came up to visit. We all went to Hannibal and rode the paddle wheeler up and down the Mississippi. Lorene was able to spend most of the day with both her children, her only close relatives who were still alive. She kept her ticket stub to remember that special day.

I managed the Travelers Hotel located in Kirksville that the church had purchased to use in Bible school. The second floor had twenty-six rooms we rented to the public. Lorene had stayed in the hotel many years ago when Earl had plastered the Telephone Building there in town. I chose adjoining rooms and Sherry and Lorene and I had a nice meal in the hotel dining room and she again stayed in the old Travelers Hotel.

Many in our family went to Macon to the drive-in movie and saw a double feature, one of which was Babe the Pig. We had lawn chairs, blankets, snacks and sat on the ground or on the hood of the car. We had a grand time.

She would say, "I want to go to Alba's," who lived approximately 300 miles south in Galena, Missouri. Within a few hours we would be on the way to south Missouri. A week or two later we would get a call, "I want to come home" and back we would go to bring her back home. I still don't miss the audio tapes, Tarzan of the Apes, she liked to listen to as we traveled. Zane Grey was one of her favorite authors. If she held the book just right with good light she could read.

Word puzzles helped her spend much of her day along with an ongoing battle with the squirrels that invaded the bird feeder installed at her window. She would knock on the window but the squirrel wouldn't budge. They would just continue to eat the food placed for her birds.

She wrote personal letters to several of the grandchildren (she died before she got around to all) sharing her heart. Bible study, each evening before we went to bed, become the norm. Using the Living Bible, I would read a chapter at each setting. Her demeanor changed the last few years she lived with us. As I would read how Israel would prosper and have good times until they began to serve other gods, she would interrupt my reading and say, "What in the world is wrong with those people? Can't they see the blessing of God comes when they serve him?" She would look forward to our evenings as we read the scriptures together. Her dad had read to her family, the Samuels, when she was a young girl.

135

The beer in the refrigerator needed to be replaced less and less frequently as time went by. She left us September 3, 1999; several cans of beer, unopened on the lower shelf in the refrigerator. I still miss her, there are tears in my eyes as I remember those times that can never be again, at least in the here and now.

Lorene was born and raised in Halltown, Missouri, Earl in Nevada, Missouri. On their wedding day Lorene was age sixteen and Earl was eight years older. On December 24, 1977 Earl and Lorene McClease celebrated fifty years of marriage. They had experienced a tragic time together when their oldest son, Darrell, had succumbed to cancer in June 1974 at an age of 42. A wife, Lavern, and six beautiful children were left without a husband and father.

Refer to (Appendix A) Sherry's family.

A side note: before Lorene moved in to live with us, she sold the house in Branson to the Osmond Brothers family who had a theater within walking distance of her house. Dad and mom Osmond would be close enough to babysit the grandchildren when their children were rehearsing for their shows.

Hoby & Moose

Hoby & Ricky Joe
August 1955

My younger brother Ricky
I moved him in with my family and he became like one of
my children. Uncle Rick was two years older than Mark.

CHAPTER 21

Lilley's landing

Sherry and I met Phil and Marsha Lilley in the church that we attended while we lived in Branson, caring for Sherry's family. They own and operate Lilley's Landing, a resort located on Lake Taneycomo. I began renting a two-story condo that would accommodate our family at Lilley's Landing for a family vacation.

For nine years Sherry and I along with all our children and grandchildren spent Memorial Day week together at Lilley's Landing. Together we enjoyed fishing, boating, swimming in the pool, Branson shows, Silver Dollar City, and always one special family night that included Dolly Parton's Dixie Stampede, Presley's music show, Lambert's throwed rolls and occasionally a family picnic with fried chicken and fixings from the local deli. These activities created a closeness. That closeness comes out in all forms to warm my heart.

A Special Gift from Shelley

I don't wear being a veteran on my sleeve for all to see, although I am glad, I served my country. I'm glad I did it and I'm also glad it's over. My daughter showed me a high honor. For one Father's Day Shelley with Sherry's help, found my old Air Force personnel file and with that information paid to have my name added to the Adair County Veterans Memorial there in Kirksville, Missouri.

Later, I enrolled and completed the Master Gardener class sponsored by the University of Missouri in Columbia. Those with the designation as "Master Gardeners" maintained flower beds and other landscaped areas in the city as community service. One of my service activities was maintaining the grounds at the Veterans memorial and I proudly took my friends and showed them.

His name was Paul, we effectually called him Sack and also, Pete by his friends

Sack

The calendar time was middle to late 1920s when a young boy approached the home of Luther and Della Youngblood needing food and place to sleep. There was evidence of physical mistreatment visually on his body. Physically small and under developed due to mental retardation, he never developed mentally beyond age 5 or 6. He was no longer tolerated nor wanted by his immediate family. He was the product of incest.

My grandparents, uncles and aunts, called him Sack and he was welcomed as a member of the already seven children in Luther and Della Youngblood's family. He didn't know his given name, we later learned he was named Paul Snowden. He never spoke of his natural family, it was as if he had no memory of his mother or father, they didn't seem to exist. As I grew up in my family, he was Sack.

As he adjusted to his new surroundings it became evident that he preferred to be out-of-doors. He liked doing farm chores. He enjoyed working around the barn, working with farm animals and was good feeding them and moving them from one pasture to another but he really liked to milk the cows. He enjoyed working outside in the garden; he liked planting, hoeing, weeding and harvesting the vegetables.

He never progressed socially and couldn't relate or hold a conversation with just anyone except a family member. He never learned to read or write; his prized possessions were tools, such as a

140

potato fork and garden hoe. He was especially proud of a new ax that he could use to cut wood for the stove.

Sack lived with that family until grandma Della died in 1962 and later that year grandpa died. Grandpa Luther, before his death asked my father to take Sack into our family. I had left home and joined the Airforce 1955 and married in 1956. My sister Cleota had married and moved to New York state, and my brother Max moved to California. Sack joined my parents' family that consisted of Mom and Dad, Rick and Lavonna who were still at home. My dad died in 1978, Rick had joined my personal family in Kirksville, Missouri and Lavonna had graduated from college, married and left home, leaving my elderly mother to care for him. When mother was in her mid to late 80's, washing his cloths and cooking for him was too much of a burden. I encouraged her to call the state and discontinue caring for him.

She was receiving a small check for his care with which she had purchased a burial policy to use for his funeral. Sack spent his later years in a nursing home in Branson, Missouri. He was frequently visited by family members who came home for a visit. The family thought that Sack and my mother had been born near the same year. If this date of birth was correct, he had lived 90 years. He died of pancreatic cancer, was cremated and buried as Paul 'Pete' Snowden in 2005, at Cedar Valley Cemetery Hollister, Missouri. Mother died at age 92 and was buried in 2007.

The following article was written by my brother Max who, like me, grew up with Sack and Used by his permission.

Legend of an Old Tater Fork.
by Max Youngblood

His birth name was Paul but people who knew him, called him Pete. He grew up with the Youngblood family at Ridgedale Missouri, a small community about a mile from the Arkansas border in southern

141

Missouri. Born out of wedlock, with a speech impairment, his mother and family did not want anything to do with him.

At that time, he was thought to be mentally retarded; So, at a young age Pete was turned into an outcast and homeless person. He was ridiculed and mocked by his peers at a time in his young life that should have been the Golden Years. When my grandfather first met him and saw the living conditions he was trying to survive in, decided right then and there that Pete was going to be a permanent part of the Youngblood family.

He was a colorful character. His love was working outdoors. Vegetable gardens were his favorites. In the spring when everything ripened, he enjoyed showing everyone things that he had picked. His favorite past time was digging new potatoes. His most prized possession was a (tater fork) as he called it, which was used to dig new potatoes. He never worried about money, bills, taxes or current events, he enjoyed living in his own private world of simple and beautiful things. So, you see I would never call Pete mentally retarded because in his small world of limited knowledge the things he loved to do were done well.

I grew up with Pete, and when Granddad died, he came to live with our family. Dad and mom built him his own private house where he lived until his health got so bad that he had to move to a home where he could get professional care. Pete and I spent a lot of time in the woods. I thought he could talk to the wild animals because they were never afraid of him. He would spot a deer or squirrel before I ever knew that they were there. His constant companion was an old homeless dog that dad had picked up somewhere wandering down the road.

In his later years, he would often go down into a hollow and couldn't climb back up. So I would have to help him. He loved to cut down small trees with an ax. After the branches were all cleaned up, he would stack them in big piles ready to be cut up for firewood. They were a prized possession he would show everybody. He never forgot

142

a name. When introduced to him for the first time you would never forget his name either.

He was always doing things to make you laugh. Mom was working outside in the yard one day; she heard a racket coming from his house and decided to investigate and see what he was up to. There he was, singing a song and dancing. He sure was happy. He loved to chew tobacco. He would tell everyone, "I was born in a 'baccer' (tobacco) patch".

Pete never asked for much out of life, just a kind word, something to eat and a place to lay his head. I am thankful I had the privilege of knowing him. He was one of the last true Legends of the Ozark mountains that will always be remembered with a smile when folk lore is discussed. Nature has now reclaimed the wood pile he created, old animal friends weep at his passing, his (tater fork) stands in the corner of the shed gathering rust from lack of use and the old lawnmower he used to cut the lawn with is silent, never to run again.

Pete's in heaven now, free of pain and reunited with the family that loved him so much. A true Legend is a special person like Pete that only come around once in a lifetime. It's always hard to give them up. But I know God puts these special people on earth for a purpose and will never tolerate abuse or let them suffer too much. He will always find them a safe haven with families that treat their disabilities with love, not scorn. Pete, you were my friend. May the sun always shine bright on your new home and your vegetable garden be blessed with an abundance of fruit, may your (tater fork) stay bright and shiny. You were such an important part of my life and to all others that knew you. I will never forget.

God, Bless You, Rest in peace my friend.

Your Pal Max

Uncle Buford and Sack
Buford was the youngest of Luther and Della's children

CHAPTER 22

I Lost the Love of My Life

Sherry's scheduled mammogram revealed a lump. With the diagnosis of carcinoma came the possibility of the word "terminal" becoming a reality. True to her character she was concerned more with my wellbeing than her own. If I don't survive this, I want you to find someone and marry again. I later learned she had also shared the same desires for me with our girls. She did beat the cancer but her life ended much too soon; she passed away two years after we relocated to our childhood home in south Missouri.

"Hobert, do you want me to die?" Sherry asked. The question startled me. " No, of course not, I don't want you to die!" I spoke. Then, I began to realize my wife of sixty-one years was thinking about death and wondering how I would feel if she did. "Honey, are you thinking of dying and do you want to die?" I asked.

"No, I don't want to die," she said, "but you never know."

I had taken her from her home, out of the Ozark mountains to Wyoming, Washington DC, Virginia, Conroe, and Houston, Texas, whale watching in Boston, Massachusetts, Alaska and finally, in her later years, back home to the Ozark Mountains where she was again around her old friends and family. Our marriage covenant had stayed intact.

Sherry had a pacemaker, she was a breast cancer survivor, she'd had both knees and a hip replaced which had left her in almost

145

constant pain and limited her mobility. Her heart was giving out, she was retaining water, her kidneys were not operating at an acceptable level, and her blood oxygen level was low. Hospital and skilled nursing treatments are applicable only for someone on the mend. Sherry was maintaining her condition, but not improving. She would have to be transferred to a nursing home. Hospice was our answer.

They equipped a room in Susie and Stan's house in Aurora with equipment needed to care for Sherry. Tracy, Susie and Shelley were around-the-clock with their mother. Julie was there every time she could and always brought a ray of sunshine of God's Spirit as she played the piano and sat with her mother

"Have you talked to God about dying?" I spoke.

"No," she said.

"Honey," I said, "talk with God about this; ask Him what He wants you to do? I will go along with whatever you guys decide. Though it is not my personal desire for you to die, let's see what His will is for you." This conversation occurred on Friday morning, and later that day she became unresponsive.

That evening I returned to Cassville to sleep in my bed and returned early the next morning back to her bedside. Her medication had taken effect, she was sleeping very comfortable, but she no longer communicated with us. I sat with her a while. She was very peaceful and quiet. I went back home to Cassville to do some neglected housekeeping. During that afternoon, she became restless and the girls heard her say out loud, "I don't want to die."

Later that evening she again became restless and the three girls began to sing to her.

"When I'm down, when I'm down and out, when my heart is filled with fear and doubt, I just lift up my head and He lifts up my heart and my burdens just all roll away. Roll 'em all away Lord ...."

A tear fell from the corner of her eye. After a while she became calm and the girls, who sat with her in shifts, decided who would get some rest. Susie and Shelley went to bed and Tracy continued sitting with her. Sometime after 11 pm Tracy moved over near her and began to tell her "Mom, I love you. Heaven is waiting. Our Father is waiting for you there. We will miss you terribly, but we will all be okay. You and Him do whatever you two want to do." Tracy again saw a tear roll down her face and felt a change in the room. She quickly called me to come back and the other girls to come to the room. She very calmly quit breathing. Someone said, "Did Mom just die?" Yes, she had just changed worlds.

She loved us so much she struggled between leaving us and going on to heaven and waiting for us to catch up. She chose heaven and a new body that was working properly. I would have chosen the same. I miss her so much and as I remember our years together, the good times we have enjoyed and our great family, the pain is bearable—at least for a season.

Sherry and I had an on-going disagreement that we could never solve, even at her death, and because of it we would often argue. She would always try to prefer me and I would try to prefer her. It was very difficult to pick a place to eat or where to go on an evening car ride. Our conversations would often go like this:

"Where do you want to go eat?" I would say. "Where do you want to go eat?" she would say. "I asked you first," I would say. "I know, but I don't care, so you pick." "What kind of food do you want?" I would ask. "What kind do you want?" "Oh! Come on just tell me where to go!" I would say. "Let's go wherever you want." "Sherry, you are the most stubborn individual I know." "Yes, I know, I know I am the worst you have ever seen. Now where do you want to go?" and on and on and on. I really miss those arguments.

Ripples on the Pond

When just a young boy, I spent time throwing rocks in our farm pond and watching the ripples go out in all directions, and then end when they reached the water's edge. Life is like a ripple that starts somewhere in the middle of the pond and travels until it reaches the shore. Someone or something probably motivated you as you started your life's pursuit of purpose. In 1950, a thirteen-year-old girl, without

147

knowing it at the time, threw a rock in my pond starting ripples going out in all directions.

My two-room country school was closing and I would be attending high school in Hollister, Missouri. I was seated on the stage of my soon-to-become-new-school, graduating from the eighth grade, and this girl seated in the second row behind me was also graduating. There was no chemistry, not love at first sight; in fact, I was just savoring the moment. I was to speak at the graduation and was seated on the front row with the school board members. This girl and some of her cousins were seated behind me and, being the new boy in town, I was receiving all the attention from the girls - and I liked it.

She had a typical upbringing in the Missouri Ozarks. Her family, like mine, were poor - but we didn't know it. Her father, like mine, had to leave the family in the summer and go where the work was. And, she had spent much of her young life with her brother, sister and mother. She has shared with me stories of hours spent playing in the hay loft of their barn, and an old horse that she often rode. She spoke of the times spent playing with cousins in a creek that ran through their property, and roaming the hills in Taney County, Missouri of their family farm. She has a tremendous love for her family and, with fondness, related the altercations with her older brother, Darrel, who would start a friendly fight by picking on her. She would be mad when the bus came for school, and so, would take her time walking down to the bus. Asa Groves would be yelling through the bus window, "Come on, Sherry, we don't have all day!"

Her life almost ended at eight years old when her appendix ruptured filling her abdomen with poison. She hovered between life and death - there were questions if she would recover. The hospital chaplain, a catholic priest, came and prayed for her and she received a miracle - she was physically healed. Her life and the life of her immediate family changed; they had a more intense reverence toward God.

Our high school years had lots of good times and memories: lots of friends; basketball and softball games; school plays; band and music festivals. Turning sixteen and being able to drive the family car made a great difference in my love life. Sherry and I began to spend time together, especially in our sophomore, junior and senior years of school. Our class raised enough money, making fudge candy and selling it at ballgames, that we twelve seniors took a trip to the Gulf Coast prior to graduation. It became too apparent that 'she was the one'. She stole my heart; really, God did something in my life that I just couldn't live without her.

Five years had passed since I met her at our eighth-grade graduation. Four years of high school and one year of college later, on January 10th, 1956, she agreed and became Mrs. Hobert Youngblood. The small wave I am calling 'my life' continued to move toward the shore.

My decision to turn my life over to the Lord was the result of Sherry recommitting her life to the Lord at a meeting she attended with my mother. Her encounter with the Lord thirteen years earlier become deeper. I knew she had made a quality decision. God had been dealing with me for several years and I knew now was the time to become a Christian, and so, I did.

Since our marriage, I watched this teenage bride change into an accomplished individual. She became an excellent wife, mother and homemaker. She mastered the ability of caring for a large family with no one, including her husband, ever feeling neglected. She later managed a major medical office with ten providers and thirty-five employees. She has been, and still is, an excellent role model. Our children all love the Lord and are/have instilled in their children the love and respect for God. Our life together has spanned over sixty years, six children, nineteen grandchildren and seventeen great-grandchildren. She was instrumental in seeing her husband, our children, and both her parents turn wholeheartedly to God.

Proverbs 31:28 (NKJV) [28] Her children rise up and call her blessed; Her husband *also,* and he praises her. *(This has and is happening - God is so good.)*

149

post script: After 61 years of marriage, she left me and went to heaven. 1-29-2017; the ripples have now reached the pond bank!!!

Hobert, Mark, born May 1957 Steve, born Nov.1958

CHAPTER 23

My Second Marriage

With Sherry gone, I found solace with my family and other friends. I reconnected with several high school friends, still living in the area when I attended my high school reunion. Kay Simmons and two longtime friends had visited Sherry and me when she learned we had moved back to the Ozarks. She was walking but still showing signs of the trauma from an auto accident that had almost taken her life. Sherry and I had followed her recovery by reading the daily accounts posted on Facebook by Sandy her daughter. Our families had attended church together in the mid-1960s and she babysat for us. Sherry named Susie our fourth child and 2nd daughter Susanne Kay after her.

Several months later I was at a loss of what to do with myself and I went for a drive. While on the road I remembered Kay's visit a year and half earlier, and called her and then dropped by to check on her recovery progress. We were sitting on her porch, her coffee was terrible, and I stayed maybe fifteen or twenty minutes and found her to be very lonely also. We decided to stay in contact. A few weeks later I drove over to her home and we had lunch together. During that time, we decided to attend a Branson show.

We both were resolute, we were not looking for a mate, no intention of marriage, let's just hang out and be friends. It never entered my mind that she would one day be my bride. After a few weeks I began to realize that I had deep feelings for her but kept them

151

suppressed. Had you asked me if I had feelings for her, I would have told you no.

I had purchased nonrefundable airline tickets for a California visit to see Max my brother. Kay had tickets to Virginia to be with her daughter Kathy for Christmas. The day before I was scheduled to leave, we spent eleven hours together. I brought the subject of marriage up and asked her, "I don't think this will ever happen, but just theoretically if I were to ask you to marry me what would you say?"

"Are you proposing to me?" she said.

"No! I'm just wondering."

After a long pause, she said, "I probably would say yes."

Realizing how we both felt about the other, I knew that a marriage was possible. We spent the balance of the day together talking about all the possibilities and we prayed together, asking God if we were to even be married. We asked God to strengthen our friendship but take away how we felt about each other if marriage was not His perfect will for us.

Over sixty years ago I asked Sherry McClease to become my wife. Standing before God we made a covenant to love, honor and protect one another until death; I had kept my vow to her.

I had no reservation when I asked Kay to become my wife and she accepted. It was not like we had just met; our families had been entwined in one way or another for several years. We told our children that we planned to be married, but we didn't know when.

When I returned from California, Kay picked me up at the airport, we discussed several dates for our marriage but made no final decision. We both agreed we would not have an elaborate ceremony, no public wedding, just a simple exchanging of vows and then announce it to the family.

I went to bed asking God for help in our decision. In the early hours of the morning God directed me to read the story of Isaac. That account said when they brought Rebekah to him and she became his

152

wife then he had comfort and peace. Kay brings me contentment, purpose and peace.

We actually didn't know the date until the day of the wedding. Our marriage vows were made on December 4, 2017, in a simple ceremony officiated by my brother Rick Youngblood in the office of his church.

Hoby and Kay at Silver Dollar City

Appendix A – Sherry's Family

Earl Albert McClease, my father, was born October 20, 1903 at Schell City, Missouri. He was the third child of Pat & Chloe McClease. He had eight siblings. His Father, Pat, was a construction laborer, along with being a farmer and other jobs. He was gone from home a lot, going where the work was, leaving Chloe and the children to fend for themselves. I never heard my dad say anything bad about him and his wandering ways, but did get a few hints from my aunts that my granddad was sort of a gad-about and made life hard for his family at home. I did hear dad say that he and his older brother George, often hunted rabbits, squirrel or even possum, so the family would have meat to eat. I thought he was kidding me for a long time, but realized it was the truth.

My dad was very much a family person. He felt a lot of responsibility toward all of them. I feel sure it was because of the way his mom raised him. He always referred to her, affectionately as mom. She depended on the older children to assist her with the chores and help put meat on the table, and with the family income.

Earl attended school on and off for eight years, and told me he went to the eighth grade three times. I am not certain, but I think it was because the high school was in another town, and he was needed at home and could not afford to go live away at that time. His outstanding class was Math. He could figure out nearly any problem and arrive at the correct answer, even college Algebra. Sherry, my older sister, must have inherited some of that math ability, and I wish

I had. Not sure about Darrell, our brother, but he was able to figure blueprints and bid jobs, so he must have been pretty good at it, too.

Dad always talked a lot about his grandma McClease, she seemed to be very special to him. He spent time with her and she was a big influence in his life. Chloe's Mother had died when she was a girl, and she had lived with her Aunt Rose, so he was not around his grandparents very much. When Earl was fifteen, he and Velma (his older sister) and her husband Wilbur, and a girl cousin, all drove out to Oregon together to find work and adventure. He worked several different jobs, including a ranch hand and a cook in a logging camp. The cousin remained in Oregon, marrying a local man. Forty years later, Dad & Mom visited them.

Dad sent most of his money home to his mom, when he decided to go home, he had just barely enough money for the trip and food. But did manage to buy a white silk shirt for himself. Velma & Wilbur had returned to Missouri previously, as she was pregnant and ill.

He rode the train; in a town somewhere in Kansas, there was a layover between trains, he ran into his father. They visited awhile, and before they parted, Pat asked if he had any money, and took most of Dad's cash, leaving him little to eat on. Dad returned home, as George was also out West somewhere, and he was needed at home.

When Dad grew to a young man, his family moved to Springfield, Mo. He became acquainted with some young men who were plasterers, and he learned the plastering trade. It was hard, heavy work, but Earl was good at it, and he became expert on the finish work. He became lifetime friends with Guy Jeffery. They worked and roomed together throughout Oklahoma, Missouri, Arkansas, and anyplace else they found work and adventure.

Dad was working in Oklahoma in 1927, and his family was now living near Halltown, Missouri. It was there that he met his wife to be, Lorene Samuels. His two sisters, Ruby and Emogene, were attending high school and he went there to see them on one of his trips home and Lorene spied him. Earl was 24 and Lorene was just 16 years old,

156

but she knew the first time she saw him that he was the man for her, and she told her friend just that.

 They became acquainted and when Earl came home for visits, they dated. Lorene's parents were strict with her, and understandably so, as he was eight years older and much more worldly. Her Mother was particularly uncertain of him, but her father, Am Samuels, liked him immediately. After a fairly short courtship, they were married on December 24, 1927. They drove to Springfield, with her father and Guy & Eula Jeffery as witnesses, was married by a Justice of the Peace who performed the ceremony. They then returned to stay with her folks for the remainder of the Christmas Holiday, before moving to Oklahoma, where he had a job plastering. They shared an apartment with Guy & Eula, and this suited Lorene fine, as she did not know the first thing about cooking, and Eula was a wonderful cook. They had some grand times, along with some lean and stormy ones, but survived in fine shape. Mom told of when they returned to Missouri for the first visit in three months, she talked and sang all the way home, and by the time they reached her folk's home, she had lost her voice, and could not talk at all.

During the courtship of Earl and Lorene the McClease family had moved to a farm southwest of Hollister, Missouri. The farm belonged to Rose Bender, Chloe's aunt. She made an agreement with them that if they would live and farm the place, and provide her with a home and care for the remainder of her life, the farm would be theirs. The farm was about five rocky, rough miles from Hollister, with barely trails to drive on, but it was their home from that time on. It was located in a small valley, with a creek running through it, and nice fields for cutting hay and raising crops, along with orchards and garden spots. As I remember it was a 200-acre farm. It was the end of Pat's wandering days, and Grandma Chloe loved the place. It was her first real permanent home since her early childhood.

Earl & Lorene lived in several places for the next year or so, then the Depression and Darrell came along. Darrell was born in September, 1931, at the YMCA Camp in Hollister, Missouri. Most of the family lived close, except for a sister named Okla who married Andy Shelton and moved away from this area along with Velma & Wilbur.

I recall my parents talking about living with the McClease family during the depression. The construction business had come to a halt, and Earl drove a truck to make a living. I asked my mom about living with the whole family, and she loved it. The men would get out and do the chores, cut the wood for the heat and cooking, and the women would do the laundry together, cook plenty of food, but with all the garden food, fruit from the orchard, pork from the hogs butchered, the food was plentiful. They pooled their money for the things they could not grow, such as tobacco, coffee and sugar, etc. Gas and sugar were rationed, but they made do. They would play cards and games in the evenings and did not feel they were bad off at all.

When business started back up, Earl resumed plastering, and Lorene & Darrell went along to where ever he had to go to find work. Sherry was born in Miami, Oklahoma, March 19, 1937. Lorene developed yellow jaundice and was very sick for a long time. Earl moved her to Halltown, to be close to her family and they could help her with the children, and he would come home when he could to see them. This started the era of working away from home, just seeing the family occasionally.

Sometime during 1940, Earl and his family moved to California to work. When they returned home Earl and George started a pottery business, located at George & Agnes' home, near the McClease home. Alba Lynn was born at George's home on August 1, 1941. The two families were living together at the time until Earl completed the house, he was building close to the two farms. Agnes had given birth to a son a few weeks earlier, and he was gravely ill. Mom always felt guilty about me being so healthy and loud, with the baby Larry being

158

so frail and sick. He died shortly after. They remained in the pottery business for several years, until George became sick and died suddenly with cancer of the brain. I don't know how much longer the business kept operating but Earl went back into the plastering business.

Earl started working for D.C. Snead, a plastering contractor out of Tulsa, Oklahoma. Soon he was named foreman and ran many jobs for Mr. Snead. In the early 50s, they became business partners, along with another man from Tulsa, Oklahoma, who ran the office. They did big buildings, such as hospitals, and the large oil buildings located in Tulsa, involving a year or more to complete.

Earl & Lorene borrowed money against their home at Hollister to be able to buy into the plastering corporation. Lorene was against it, but it soon was paid back and the money became good. Earl always liked to drive new automobiles, and bought an Oldsmobile and a Buick. He also renovated the 4-room house into a 3-bedroom house, with large airy rooms. The kitchen was very large with windows all across the front, and he never wanted curtains on that window. He spent most of his time at home sitting in the kitchen, visiting with Lorene while she prepared meals, or playing cards with all of the family. Most weekends we had company either to play cards or for Sunday dinner. Dad never broke ties with his family, our home was always a busy, fun place to be for his siblings and their families.

When Dad had jobs away from home, which they all were, he would drive home on Friday nights, and leave again on Sunday afternoons. He rented a small apartment or room, sometimes with my cousin, Pat McClease, George's son, who often worked for Earl as a plasterer. We had a barn, and Lorene and Darrell milked cows, along with Earl. They sold off the milk cows about the time I was 6 or 8, as it was quite a hassle for Darrell & mom to milk, with Darrell going to school and being on the basketball team. I never learned to milk a cow, and don't regret that at all. We still had chickens, pigs, and some stock cows, and Darrell had a horse he named Fanny. We never had a telephone the entire time we lived at Hollister, but if there was an emergency, people contacted Bob & Emogene Hulland and they

159

would drive out and deliver the message. Mom did not drive much when I was small but when Darrell turned 16 and got a car, she began to drive knowing that when Darrell was gone from home, she would be able to get around. During the summer months, after school was out, we often went with dad and stayed until time to go back to school. We stayed in a trailer court in Vinita, Oklahoma. the year I turned 10, and that was the summer I will always think back to as a favorite one. I had other kids to play with, and I learned to ride a bicycle. I never owned one, as we lived on a curvy, hilly road, and dad thought it was too dangerous, he was probably right, but I always wanted one. I also had my first and only real birthday party that year. One summer, we lived at Benton, Arkansas, another at Muskogee, Oklahoma, etc. We lived in Springfield, Missouri for a short part of my 4th grade, and Sherry and I attended St. Agnes Catholic School, and we walked. We lived in an apartment house, on Elm Street. The rooms were very large, but it was a dimly lit, cold building, and I never felt at ease there. Lorene was sick then, and had a complete hysterectomy right after school was over, at Skaggs Hospital, Branson, Missouri. I was not allowed to see her for 10 days, as they did not allow children under 12 on the floor she was on, and back then, they kept patients much longer than they do now.

Dad taught Darrell the plastering trade, and he worked for a year or more after he graduated from Hollister School in 1949, then he joined the Air Force, as the Korean War broke out, and he chose to enlist rather than be drafted. He was stationed in west Texas during boot camp, and I remember we made several trips to see him, and LaVern Quick went with us, as Darrell and she had been dating since he was in high school. Darrell & LaVern were married in May, 1952, and lived in Albuquerque, New Mexico. until he was sent overseas to Korea, and she was pregnant with their first child, Darra. LaVern spent a lot of time at our home before and after the baby was delivered, to all our joy.

My Granddad McClease died in 1953, of stomach cancer. He had surgery, but never did any good afterwards. I remember he was in bed most of the time, and I was too shy to go around him much. Dad was home at the time he died, and mom was right there with him until the end. I missed him a lot, but I am sure it was devastating to my father. He had to be gone so much, and now felt responsible for his mom and Aunt Rose, too.

When I was about 5 years old, which would have been 1946, dad started taking us three kids to the Catholic Church in Branson, Missouri. At first, Lorene refused to go, but after a time began going with us. She was not comfortable about going to a Catholic Church, as she had always heard bad things about them. The priest was Father Farrell, and he spent a lot of time at our house, giving us instructions and teaching us about the Catholic religion. Father Farrell had long since retired from actively being a parish priest, he assisted in the funeral when dad died 45 years later. He had always been available for the McClease Family. We all were baptized at the Lady of the Lake Church at the same time. Most of the McClease family, except Velma, living in the Branson/Hollister area joined the Catholic Church.

Earl was always an avid hunter and fisherman. He loved to fly fish on Long Creek, a few miles from home at Hollister, Missouri, until the Table Rock Dam covered it with lake water, and hunted deer in the Ozark hills, usually coming home with one or two, whatever the law allowed for that season. Darrell loved to hunt too, and usually was successful in bagging a deer. Earl and Lorene started going to Colorado during the deer and elk seasons, and went several years in a row, always coming home with wild game. He hunted squirrels and rabbits and quail, and loved to hunt duck. Our meals were often venison, elk, squirrel, and quail. I never thought any more about sitting down to the wild meat than I did beef or pork. Earl bought a jeep and pulled it behind him to Colorado, often through snowy passes and steep drop-offs. They rented a cabin that was warmed with wood heat, and cooked on a wood stove, and enjoyed it all. Mom usually went out in the jeep with Earl, but never did carry a gun. They both talked about those trips often, and bad health was the only thing that prevented them from going later on.

161

When the White Elephant Motel and dance floor was opened up by Clarence & Ruby Gentry, dad & mom would go up there often. There was not any liquor allowed on the premises, but I am sure that they managed to drink, but they took me with them, and I was amazed to see my parents dance together. They danced together easily, and both loved it. Dad was a smooth dancer with great rhythm, and he taught me how to dance like him. He never seemed put out to dance with me, in fact, he seemed to be proud to dance with his daughters, as Sherry learned to dance from him, too. We all loved to see him do the 'Charleston', his long legs seemed to be rubbery.

(This narrative of the McClease family was taken from papers kept by my late wife Sherry and seemed to have been compiled by a younger sister. Permission to include in this book by Alba Cunningham in a telephone conversation on Thursday, May 7, 2020)

Appendix B — Bonnie Youngblood

Bonnie Youngblood, my mother was born in 1913. Her father moved so much she attended several schools and was able to graduate from the eighth grade. She was a brilliant woman with a formal education could have been a prolific writer. In her following story I have attempted to preserve her way of communication in both her speech and writing. The entire content of this appendix was taken from her own writing that she wrote by hand. My son-in-law Dave Pingel carefully edited her notes and often had conversation with her about meanings. I have attempted to use most of the same written words that she used; spelled as spoken in her every day conversation.

Aunt Bonnie, as she was affectionately called by her friends, was the daughter of George and Victoria Youngblood. George, Victoria, Bonnie and a brother Paul were instrumental in bringing a spiritual awakening to the Mountains of Kentucky, the Hills of Missouri, and the Plains of Oklahoma where many were saved and filled with the Holy Ghost in an out-pouring of the Spirit. Several churches resulting from those revivals, still stand in southern Missouri.

Converted at age 14, she traveled with her beloved "Poppy," the name she called her father. She played a foot drum in the services and was the reader of the Bible when her father preached. She later married Grover Youngblood and gave birth to six children; the first died at birth and is buried in a cemetery at Omaha, Arkansas. She pastored small churches in the Missouri Ozarks and assisted other ministries when they set up their tents or built brush arbors in the area. She didn't want a crown that was spoken of in the bible she just wanted to hear her Jesus say, "Well done, Bonnie!"

The following is her writing, sermons, and songs.

Hindrance

In Abesville, Missouri when Dad was preaching, the altars were filled every night. Men and women were praying through to old time salvation. People were so hungry for God. Two or three families would gather together, spread their suppers, and eat. Then they would all gather out on the hillsides to seek God, thinking they'd find Him and be saved. Before the service one night, a big tall man knelt at the altar in the old Abesville school house. As Dad sat by listening to him pray, this man said, "Lord, if you will save me, I'll take that log chain I stole back to its owner and I'll go to Springfield and pay that clerk for that Stetson hat I just put on and walked out with." Dad sat and watched and listened to him seek God and make wrongs right. Pretty soon he hit the Rock and God saved him. He took the log chain home and next day he went to Springfield. He went in the store and tried on a Stetson hat and said, "Lady, what do you get for these?" She told him. He said, "No, I don't want this one, I just want to pay you for one I put on and walked out with the other day." He said, "God saved me last night. A very happy experience indeed."

My dad was a good trader, a good farmer. He was a good business man. Could have made a success at either, but he said, "God has called me preach and woe is unto me if I preach not the gospel." 1 Corinthians: 16.

One year in Davenport, Oklahoma, just this side of Davenport, he put in 29 acres of cotton. He cleared $1300.00 on 29 acres. He promised God if He would help him to make a little piece of money that year, he'd go right on preaching His Word. Sure, enough we gathered our cotton, then went out in God's service. God answered our prayers. We went on out in the gospel work with eight children in the family. It meant a big sacrifice to preach the gospel from place to place.

Dad was holding a revival in a place and there was good interest. The altars would fill with hungry souls seeking God. One certain woman would come to service and when the altar service was made, she would get in the altar and start to pray for the people seeking God. She professed to be a Christian. When she would get in and start to pray for them, the service would completely die. Everyone would wonder 'what'' wrong with the service?" Dad watched her for a few nights and when she just stayed away from the altar, people prayed through. But when she would get down to help the seekers, the service died. Dad told mom, he said, "The hindrance is with that woman that comes to church early." He said, "Vick, tomorrow evening I am going to talk to her and ask her not to get in the altar until she cleans her life up. There's something in her life that ought not to be." So, Dad and mom came early the next evening to see her before anyone else got to service. He said, "We don't want to offend her or hurt her feelings. I want to help her to get right with God." When she came in, they spoke and begin to talk about the hindrance they had in the altar service.

Dad said, "Sister, I believe it's you. There's something wrong with your life and you can hide it from men, but you and God knows it. I will have to ask you to stay out of my altar until you make it right. It is keeping these souls from praying through." She just blew up. She said, "I'll stay out and God will too." Dad said, "Sister, get in the altar when the call is made and we will help you straighten it out." She stayed out of service for three or four nights but the last week she came back. When the altar call was made, she went and sought God.

The next day she went over to her neighbor and took back some things she had stolen that was not hers. She confessed to different ones that she had did wrong and talked and said hard things about. The next night when she got in the altar,

165

God saved her and filled her with the Holy Ghost. The revival went on and was a real success

Our Great Consolation

There are thousands of things that could be written about these wonderful men and women of God, but time and space won't allow me to do so. We have written these for a blessing to all who read. These are all true to my knowing. I am the oldest daughter, the first one of the 8 children to get converted (at only 14 years of age). I traveled with my dad in the gospel work and helped him, read for him. Mother, dad, Paul and I were a quartet. We led and began the singing in our revivals. Paul, mother and me sang special songs. We had many prayer meetings in our home. Those wonderful meetings are all in the past and will never be 'till we all meet again over in the pearly white city.

Mother passed away August 1, 1946. Just a day or two before her passing, I stood by her one afternoon. She said, "Bonnie, I am going to leave this old, unfriendly, world. I'm going home." Dad was so heartbroken. He felt like his life was nearly ruined. He went back to Siloam Springs, mother's home town. He later married Sister Bea Thompson; a lady that had gotten saved in their meetings years ago. He lived in Siloam Springs until his death. He preached to all his neighbors and friends at every opportunity. He suffered three strokes. Brother Bob Grady and I went down one day to pray for him when he had his last stroke. As we prayed, the power of God came down. He said to Brother Grady, "If God don't heal me, I am ready to go, but I am trusting God all the way." When we got ready to leave, Brother Grady said, "Brother Youngblood, if I don't see you anymore, when you get over there, if you go over before I do, you look for me for I'll be there." So, on March 16, 1955 Dad went away to be with mother in their new home that they had worked so hard for. He trusted God to the end. He never wavered in his faith one bit. Brother Deward Watson came and prayed for him two or three times, but God took him on home. Powell died at the age of 95 years 8 months and so many days. He was born in DeKalb County, Missouri. Bethina and Powell are buried side by side in the little cemetery at Seneca, Missouri. Dad is buried at Siloam Springs in the big cemetery right across from the John Browns University. On his tombstone it reads, "Gone but not forgotten. In the service of our Lord 40 years." Mom is buried at Omaha, Arkansas in the little graveyard just below the lonesome pines. At the time of death, arrangements could not be made to put them side by side. Uncle Jerry and Aunt Tildia are buried in Oklahoma not far from Turkey Ford, near Miami, Oklahoma. Alta and Elia are buried in Seneca, Missouri. Lula is buried in California. Grover's mom and dad are buried in the Cedar Valley graveyard. Lula and Alta Standley, Powell's daughter, passed away a few years ago. Their son, Johnie, passed away, too. He was living in Carthage, Missouri. They were all living for God, living true Christian lives, trusting in the old time God who never changes but is the same yesterday, today, and forever. George's children are all living but one; a little twin girl, Lula, passed away December 12, 1952. In Jenkins, Kentucky George had 4 sons, Clyde, Paul, Phillip and Sylvanus. All Christians but 2 sons. 3 daughters, Bonnie, Jessie, and Lois still living. All Christians. One son, Paul, is a minister. One daughter, Bonnie, a minister. One great consolation we younger generations (Clyde passed. away in 1974) have is this, Haggai 2:6-9: "This is what the LORD Almighty says: "In a little while I will once more shake the heavens and the earth, the sea and the dry land. I will shake all nations, and the desired of all nations will come, and I will fill this house with glory" says the LORD Almighty. 'The silver is mine and the gold is mine,' declares the LORD Almighty. 'The glory of this present house will be greater than the glory of the former house,' says the LORD Almighty. 'And in this place, I will grant peace,' declares the LORD Almighty."

Revelation 22: 14, "blessed are they that do His commandment." Revelation 22: 20, "He which testifieth these things saith, Surely I come quickly. Amen. Even so, come, Lord Jesus."

"I'm Just Getting Started"

I remember when the revised version of the Bible came out. There was a salesman selling in Siloam Springs where my father was living. Dad reached for the old King James Version and began to hunt out the blood pages where to him meant more. They had been changed in the revised version. He began to preach to the salesman over in Revelation 2: 2 where it said 'if any man taketh away from the words of the book of this prophecy, God would take his part out of the Book of Life Revelation 2: 2, and out of the Holy city. He said, "Brother, I wouldn't let you leave this version in my house. I'll just keep the old book I have. When God saved me, he gives me something to tell. I've worked at it 40 years and I still can't get it told. I've been trying to tell it ever since and seems to me I'm just getting started."

Another time, in Kentucky, my oldest brother had rheumatism so bad he lay in the bed. His knees were drawed together. His legs wanted to lie crossed all the time. His fingers were drawed. His toes were drawn 'til he was a real invalid. My mother and father anointed him with oil and claimed God promises. God wonderfully healed him, straightened every finger and toe and his legs and made him whole in every way. Again, God proved He was the Master.

In every little business we ever had, Dad would preach to everyone, salesman and all. People would say, "Brother George, you'll ruin your business preaching to everyone."

He said, "Well, I don't want no business I can't tell people about God. If preaching will ruin it, God will help me make it some other way. Just let it be ruined. I'll move on."

One time he was at a big fellowship meeting and the ministers were supposed to wear little badges and all sit together, grouped in one place. When they brought the badge to Dad, he said, "What's that for?"

And the man said, "Brother Youngblood, to show your colors."

And he said, "Give mine to someone else. I've got enough salvation to show mine."

He never liked to be called Reverend. He always said, "I'm not reverend, I'm just plain George. Never felt worthy of no honor." He always said God saved him out of hell and it would take all the rest of his days working, without no honors, he just wanted to preach a risen Savior to the souls of men.

One-time Dad went to Forsyth, Missouri with Ollie White and Bob Jones and there was a man preaching in the yard by the old Court House. This man was fighting old time Pentecost and the way Dad saw the Bible.

This man said, "Now there was old Uncle Powell Youngblood. He was a good old man, but he was way wrong. He and his boy, George, brought the gospel to this country, but the Lord has given us different light than they had." And he begins to try to prove his points.

Dad was sitting there in the car listening. Pretty soon as the man finished, dad slid out of his coat and walked out in the courtyard and said, "Well, I'd like to testify too." The crowd was still standing, grouped. Dad said, "This old Uncle Powell Youngblood that this man spoke about. Well," he said, "he was my father and, his boy, well, I am the boy.'"

He began the old story about how wicked his father and he had been and how God sent old Brother John James to Siloam and how they changed. Then he went back to Genesis and

169

ended up in Revelation and said the plan of salvation was right when it started and they had all got saved by it. He said, "Do you think God would let us all go on and be deceived for 40 years, then show us a new light? I'll tell you. No! Jeremiah 6: 16 said 'continue in the old paths.'" And when he quit preaching all the court house men were out listening to the Word of God. He told how God had sent the Holy Ghost, why he would send him, and he did and he's here today. When he finished, he thanked them for their kind attendance. When he looked around the other preacher had gone.

Ollie White said, "George, he left one hour ago." George went on his way rejoicing.

Lunatics, Devil-Possessed, and the Master

Dad and Powell established many churches over the states and counties where they preached and baptized. It's been over 50 years now since they brought the gospel to Center Point and Cedar Valley. There was Powel and his family, Dad and his family, Uncle Jerry (Powel's brother) and Aunt Tilda, who came to Cedar Valley. There were over 100 converts in the two meetings there. Men and women met out on the hillsides to pray. All night vigils were going up before God. People were bringing their lost before God. They would get burdens for people and go out and get them to the house of God. I couldn't count all the men and women who made ministers in their meetings, but I'd be safe in saying hundreds, good ministers, lots have passed away. I remember Dad and Brother R. E. Winsett of Dayton, Tennessee held revivals together. Brother Winsett was a wonderful man of God. He always let my father have all books for his revivals at cost. He contributed lots to God's cause.

My father was kneeling behind me when I got saved. He was lost away in God praying for me. He said he saw the Lord

170

dressed in white come over and lay his hand on me and on a boy that was kneeling by me. When he did, God saved me.

A man was brought to Dad's service one time who was a real lunatic. God saved him and called him to preach. He made a wonderful preacher. God put a real mind in him and he was a real attractive preacher, zealous for God; went about holding revivals, people getting saved. Another time a real devil-possessed man was brought to service. He was an invalid and said he wanted to be saved. He'd sit through service and froth would just run out of his mouth. After service Dad and two of the other men laid their hands on him, commanded the evil Spirit to go in the name of Jesus of Nazareth and the evil spirit left the man. In leaving, the man tore up the wheelchair. The devil tore him and he was dead, seemingly. They laid their hands on him and God healed him and he was one happy man, just leaping and praising God. God again proved that he was the Master.

One-time Dad went into a church to hold a revival when short dresses were in style. At the front of the church was a curtain stretched just below the pews in the front. The first thing Dad noticed was the curtain. He said, "Isn't it a shame that God's people don't have enough salvation to wear enough clothes so that they have to put up a curtain to hide their nakedness." It wasn't over 3 or 4 nights the pastor took the curtain away and God begin to pour His Spirit in that church and set it on fire. When we accept the real truth and take away the curtains, God can use us. Jesus took down the curtains and we have free access to the throne of Grace.

Another time, Dad was holding a revival at Abesville, Missouri, over by Galena. He was having a wonderful revival. Men and women were getting saved. Some boys outside had a real gang fight. Rocks were thrown. Three or four men came to our altars drunk. We knelt by them and began to pray. They made quite a little disturbance, so someone had them arrested. There must have been 10 or 12 of them. Dad and mom were subpoenaed to appear at their trial. When Dad was asked to

171

take the stand, the Judge said, "Mr. Youngblood, will you swear to tell the truth?"

He said, "Judge, I don't swear. I'll affirm the truth. I can tell you the truth without swearing. I've not took an oath since God saved me." So, he affirmed the truth rather than swearing to it.

The Judge said, "Did these 10 boys here disturb your meeting?"

Dad answered, "No, these boys didn't disturb me at all. Judge, I came to Abesville to get them saved, not to cause them to pay fines or get into trouble."

Their faces lit up. They were proud. Dad went on, "Those boys are good boys. They just need God to make them real citizens." The judge turned them loose.

Dad told them, "I just want everyone to come to my meeting and if one feels conviction go up his heart, I want him to pile in that old altar and give his life and heart to God." Dad declared, "Judge, I've not had a man arrested for disturbing since I've been preaching. My Bible says do good for evil, and having him arrested would be an eye for an eye and a tooth for a tooth."

So those boys came to service the next night. Instead of them being outside, they all came inside. When service began, you could have heard a pin drop and I don't know how many of those boys found God. At one baptizing, Dad baptized 29. God honors His Word and His people if they obey His Word and not bring no disgrace on His cause. I can't even remember all the many baptizing's. Dad had lots of them. In one old sawmill pond he baptized 27 at one time and also had several other baptizing's there. One time, I especially remember one girl who was fixing to be baptized. As she neared the bank, she was weeping and crying.

Dad said, "Sister, are you sure you got prayed through?"

She said, "Brother Youngblood, I'm not plum satisfied."

Dad told her, "Sister, I don't want to baptize you until you are sure. You wait till after service tonight and come to the altar and we will pray with you some more until you get satisfied. Then we will come down and baptize you." He said, "This water won't wash your sins away. It is just an answering of a good conscience before God. I'm not out to get joiners, but converts. I don't want you to follow me, but God." After service that night, she prayed through and had a smile instead of a long face. Dad and mom and a few others went with her down to the old mill pond and she was baptized and came out a happy person.

One night we were coming home from service at Ponce de Leon. We were all in an old truck after having had a wonderful service. We were singing good songs. The old folks were under conviction, as nearly all their children had gotten saved in the revivals. When we got to the old spring right by the side of the road, we decided to just stop the truck and have a meeting right by the spring. We did just that. The old folks, mother and father of the couple that owned the truck, got saved right by the spring. Say, we had a meeting all the rest of the way home. Two brothers of the same family made wonderful ministers preaching the old-time gospel. They are still going on for God. One of the boys and his wife lived close to Ponce de Leon, and it was in the summer time. Their baby was big enough, he was crawling around over the floor. The doors were open and a copperhead snake was coiled under the dresser. This baby crawled over to where it was and picked it up. It bit his hand right in the palm. They killed the snake, jumped in the car and brought the baby to our house. Dad anointed the hand that was bitten and prayed. The little hand never did even swell. The parents brought the snake and the baby to church that night. There was the scar where its fangs went in its hand. They said, "Look what God did in our home" They said, "This baby's hand never did swell." God again proved He was the Master and that He is a good God.

One time a man came after dad to go to a place to hold a revival. This man said, "Brother Youngblood, this church is in a serious condition." He said, "People over there 'baa' like sheep and even turn

173

somersaults. I am afraid to go to church. I have a creepy feeling when I go, but we need a good preacher who is not afraid to preach the truth to straighten them out." He went on, "They even claim to be Jesus Christ and one man says he is John the Baptist."

Dad said, "Give out meeting for me on a certain night. I'll go down." So, he went down. The house was full to see the sights. Dad said he saw that the Devil had taken full control of them when he got over there. They had got off in delusions of the Devil. One man said, "Brother Youngblood, did you know you're shaking hands with Jesus Christ every day?" Dad answered, "Why, no." He said, "Well, Jesus will be crucified this time with His head hanging down." Dad picked out 3 or 4 good saints that hadn't followed off in this nonsense and said, "Now, let's band together and pray and we will do our best to get this church straightened out again. "The first night he preached, God gave him Revelation 1: 18 where Jesus said "I am He that liveth, and was dead and behold I am alive forever more." Dad began to preach and clean up that church. He told them they had left the truth. "Your hearts aren't right with God." He quoted Jude 11 to 15. He said, "People won't get into delusions if they haven't committed some kind of sin. He took his text in 2 Peter, 2nd chapter and St. John 10:4-5, where Jesus said, "My sheep will hear My voice and a stranger they will not follow." Now he said, "When these people begin to 'baa' like sheep, watch our service die. And the 'summersaults' is nothing but delusions of the Devil." He said he looked for those big men to come get him and take him out. He never preached to a bunch of people as hard and plain in all his preaching. He even called them by name. Before it was over, they had one real altar service. Those people fell in the altar and repented of their sins, confessed their lives out to God, and had one real revival. Dad felt he had helped a little church that had got over zealous and left the old path and had gotten into delusions as Jude 4: 5-6, 2 Thessaliens 2 from 9 to 15, 2 Thessalonians 2:9-15 (KJV)
9 Even *him*, who's coming is after the working of Satan with all power and signs and lying wonders, 10 And with all deceivableness

of unrighteousness in them that perish; because they received not the love of the truth, that they might be saved.

11 And for this cause God shall send them strong delusion, that they should believe a lie: 12 That they all might be damned who believed not the truth, but had pleasure in unrighteousness. 13 But we are bound to give thanks always to God for you, brethren beloved of the Lord, because God hath from the beginning chosen you to salvation through sanctification of the Spirit and belief of the truth: 14 Whereunto he called you by our gospel, to the obtaining of the glory of our Lord Jesus Christ. 15 Therefore, brethren, stand fast, and hold the traditions which ye have been taught, whether by word, or our epistle. Boys Pray Through! Dad was farming between Depew and Milfay, Oklahoma in 1925. He would have to stop traveling and preaching to keep us children in school. He had 60 acres of cotton and 40 acres of corn besides our truck patches. When the cotton got up to blooming size, I was out looking at the blooms every day. Dad was out walking between the cotton rows, praying and preaching. He'd say, "Oh Lord, I know men, women, boys and girls are lost. Just help me to get free again so I can preach Your Word." It wasn't long until the crop was gathered and we were off again. But between times, dad held revivals through the country. I remember one meeting that summer at a little place called Salt Creek Bridge. Had a wonderful service. I remember a boy who had been raised to believe God's Word like we children. He had gotten sick and his family had taken him to Arizona for his health. He got better and was now back home. It wasn't long until he got sick again. He sent for dad and mom to come pray with him. He was lost and sick. As they gathered around his bed he'd pray as they prayed, but it seemed the heavens were brass. He said, "I've heard too many good sermons. I've turned the Spirit of God away too many times." His friends had gathered around to watch him go out to meet God. "Oh!" he'd say, "I'm lost!" But dad and mom and the good saints of God just stayed day and night and prayed and wept before God. Real early one morning, at break of day, he lifted his hands as he lay on his bed and begin to get

175

desperate before God. In a few moments time, say! - the heavens opened up. The power of God came down. A poor, lost, boy had prayed a hole through the skies. God saved him. He shouted and the big tears came streaming down. He crawled out of the bed, gathered all the friends by his cot and said, "Boys, pray through. I almost waited too long. Don't do like I did." He lived 3 or 4 days after that. One morning he ate breakfast and went over to the little sink, washed his hands. "Now, I am a little tired. I'll lie down and rest." He just lay down, crossed his hands, went to sleep, not to awake until Jesus comes. A lost soul saved from burning. Goodbye, Hallelujah, I Am Gone VI. When a man with his hand lifted to 'ward heaven with his foot on the land and the sea Swears by Him that lives forever That time is no longer to be; When the rich man, the poor, and free man cry for rocks and the mountains to hide, you will hear me shout when I see him: Goodbye, Hallelujah, I am gone.Ch. Goodbye, goodbye, goodbye, Goodbye, hallelujah, I am gone. When you see Jesus coming in the sky Goodbye, hallelujah, I am gone. V2. With the voice of the great Arc Angel And the trumpet of God sounding loud; It wakes up the dead who sleep in Jesus and they all appear in the clouds. The saints who are alive and remaining Are caught up to meet happy throng. You will hear me shout as I see them; Goodbye, Hallelujah, I am gone. V3. Jesus spoke of the signs before coming Said the sea and the waves would roll; Men's hearts would fail as they wondered While heaven departed - a scroll. When seven thunders uttered their voices and this old world is just about gone, you will hear me shout as I see him: Goodbye, Hallelujah, I am gone 4. Then those who have heaped up worldly treasure with their minds on the things below Adding houses and fields with pleasure When Jesus said it not be so - Those who have heaped up these worldly treasures in the last days will be running to and fro; You will hear me shout when I see him: Goodbye, Hallelujah, I am gone VS 5. Then preachers who have preached false religion Saying people cannot live without sin and the people who have followed false doctrines Hear the words: "Depart; ye cannot enter in." Without holiness, no man can walk this highway or join in with the bright righteous throng; You will hear me shout as I see him: Goodbye, Hallelujah, I am gone. Used by Bonnie Youngblood, year unknown (Note: I don't know if this is original to Bonnie or not. Like the others, it was it was written in her hand on a sheet of paper. There is no signature on it.) Hosea's Heartache Hosea 1: 1-3 The word of the LORD that came unto Hosea, the son of Beeri, in the days of Uzziah, Jotham, Ahaz, and Hezekiah, kings of Judah, and in the days of Jeroboam the son of Joash, king of Israel. The beginning of the word of the LORD by Hosea. And the LORD said to Hosea, Go, take unto thee a wife of whoredoms and children of whoredoms: for the land hath committed great whoredom, departing from the LORD. So he went and took Gomer the daughter of Diblaim. Israel was to learn the heart of God through Hosea's tragedy. Hosea's marriage was unhappy. His wife had proved untrue and had departed from the Lord. She might not have been immoral when she first married. Perhaps it came about as Gomer fell victim to the moral looseness of the times. Perhaps the tempo in her home was too slow for her. Perhaps her husband's devotion to God became distasteful. She could have broken her marriage vows secretly at first - before finally leaving her husband and children. She may have become priestess of the goddess of Ashtoreth and given herself up to the immoralities of that heathen religion in which many in Israel had turned. Hosea was left with a broken heart; he was the broken-hearted prophet. But the blighting of his fireside joys and wrecking of his home made him God's prophet, the man God wanted him to be. Hosea was fitted to see a clearer vision of God's great love. He is the prophet of God's wounded love. Perhaps at some point Hosea looked back over his life and saw the Divine hand of God despite the heartache it brought to him. Perhaps the providential hand of God had given him a wife who proved untrue and children who were not his own. Perhaps Hosea could see God's hands in it all. And perhaps Hosea received a clearer vision of the love of God's heart than any earlier prophet. God himself had known the tragic sorrow of Hosea's heart. He himself had known the pangs of unrequited love. From his own heart wrung the cry, "How shall I give thee up?" (Hosea 11:8) So we see the breaking of Hosea's heart was the making of God's prophet. Oh love weighted down with sorrow and woe, the breaking of your heart may be the making of God's man out of you. Hosea 3: 1 The LORD said to me, "Go, show your love to your wife again, though she is loved by another and is an adulteress. Love her as the LORD loves the Israelites, though they turn to other gods and love the sacred raisin cakes. Unlike many husbands, Hosea didn't lose his love for Gomer. His love suffered but still remained despite the altered attitude of his loved one. Since leaving home, Gomer had sunk low. Then one day, Hosea found her. He found her for sale as a slave. The love he once had still surges in his soul and his heart says, "How shall I give thee up?" So, he bids and buys her back. He redeemed his unfaithful wife. Hosea 3: 2-3 "So I bought her for fifteen shekels of silver and about a homer and a lethek of barley. Then I told her, "You are to live with me many days; you must not be a prostitute or be intimate with any man, and I will live with you. "The grace of God must have looked out of Hosea's eyes after the redemption of Gomer. But the grace of God did more than enable him. Hosea's sorrow wrought in him a strength, a patience, a mercy and compassion that would have never been otherwise. He was enlightened regarding the need of his nation. He looked and saw that his own situation was not an isolated case. Abounding idolatry was infecting social life with its moral looseness. Someone must speak against the evils that were completely throughout the land. Yet in so doing, the great and mighty love of God must be known and shown. Hosea's own experiences had given him light and insight into the people's needs and the heart of God. Israel, the bride of God, was proving unfaithful, forsaking him for Baal. It was spiritual adultery. His life had taught him the lessons. What Gomer was to him, Israel was to God. God is a jealous God. Out of his yearning over Gomer Hosea could feel God's yearning over his unfaithful people. Hosea became God's mouthpiece. God wept over adulterous Israel (Hosea

11: 8): "How shall I give thee up, Ephraim? how shall I deliver thee, Israel? how shall I make thee as Admah? how shall I set thee as Zeboim? Mine heart is turned within me; my compassions are kindled together." (Adma and Zoboim were small towns in the valley of Sodom. They were destroyed along with Sodom and Gomorrah - condemned to existence as a burning wasteland of salt and sulfur.) Jesus showed out God's heart when he cried in Matt 23: 37: "Oh Jerusalem, Jerusalem, thou that killest the prophets and stonest them which are sent unto thee. How often would I have gathered thy children together, even as a hen gathered her children under her wings and ye would not." God's love wasn't just for the Israelites. John 3: 16 says "God so loved the world ... "What Gomer was to Hosea; Israel was to God. What Israel was to God, we are likewise. All sinners are slaves to sin and as unfaithful to God as Gomer was to old Hosea. But God won't leave us in our sin. Like Hosea redeeming Gomer, God bought us when we were slaves of sin. He paid the price at Calvary. We see three people dying on Golgotha. One was dying to sin; one dying in sin; but He was dying for sin. Praise God. Calvary is behind us; we are bought with a price. We know that God is in Christ reconciling the world unto himself. The Lord gave his life a ransom for many. We have turned to our own way and been unfaithful. We need to repent. When we do, we find that through redemption that is in Christ Jesus, God's full and free salvation becomes ours. Whether Gomer came into newness of life, we are not told. But in the light of God's redeeming love and grace in Christ, we know we can find new life. Whatever our past has been, with God's gracious pardon comes hope. Old things pass away and behold all things become new. Editor's Note: In looking through Bonnie's sermons (see "An Introduction" at top right of page), I ran across two nearly identical messages, both of the same title. They were written on different types of paper, with different ink - and apparently at completely different times. Each sermon, however, had small but significant parts not mentioned in the other. These different parts complimented and completed each other nicely, so I decided to merge them into one sermon. As much and as often as Bonnie preached and as much as she continuously expressed her love for God, I don't think she'd mind my doing so. In fact, I can almost hear her say with a chuckle: "Give 'em two for the price of one, Dave - twice as much God and twice the power. That'll get 'em. They sure couldn't beat that, could they!"

Rest in the Homeland

1. We often meet with trials here almost too hard for us to bear; But sweet it is to know somewhere sweet rest is waiting over there.

Chorus: There's rest in the homeland fair; Sweet rest waiting over there. There's rest for the saved and true; There's rest, sweet rest, waiting there for you.

2. The way is often steep and rough, but God's sweet presence is enough. If he is with us day by day, we will be home when ends the way.

3. Pass bravely onward day by day; rely on God to lead the way. If we will trust and follow on, we'll greet the King at morning dawn.

4. Each mile-stone brings us nearer to home; soon to the crossing we shall come. There we shall meet those we love best and have with God eternal rest.

Bonnie Youngblood, year unknown.

Sharpening the Blade

Nothing is more frustrating than to try to cut wood with a dull ax. It pays to spend some time and energy sharpening the blade before we try to chop with it. Whatever the task, we need good tools. The same is true in spiritual matters. Previous experience has taught us that we achieve more with less exertion when we employ divine power. With the moving of God's spirit, we have all that is desired. Conversions are many and genuine sinners are attracted to the places of worship. Believers are made happy and edified. Without the moving of

God's spirit, we are woefully inadequate. If we fail to see this, we are trying to do God's work with a dull ax and our energy is being squandered in a superfluity of mechanics.

To correct this condition, we must renew our purpose to keep the ax in good condition. To be successful, we must learn why it has become dull. Some of these reasons are obvious:

1. The ax has come into contact with hardened hearts. Unyielding parents who have committed the woodpile to Junior have found the ax they carefully sharpened has been used elsewhere than the chopping block. Its keen edge is gone and the nails and stones were more than a match for its delicate edge. Ministers often find their anointed sermons had fell on stony hearts (not much effect).

The saints failed to prepare themselves and had missed the blessing intended for them. Their indurate hearts prevented the axe from being able to separate the evil from the good. The cause is unbelief (Heb 3: 12,13). This is also portrayed in the resurrection picture (Mk 16:9.14). Mary Magdalene had come in the midst of their mourning. She told them He has risen. Her testimony was ignored; they believed not.

The Emmaus disciples afterwards repeated her story but were discredited. Not until Jesus appeared in person was it, they accepted the miracle of his resurrection. The Lord rebuked them for their unbelief and hardening of their hearts. Our refusal to believe the witness of others can result in this kind of a spiritual condition. We too come guilty of discounting the faithful testimonies of those who have seen and experienced.

2. The ax becomes rusty because of inactivity (no use). 1 Peter 4: 10. Every believer has been provided with some capacity for service. Minister the same one to another as good stewards of the manifold grace of God. Paul said God has supplied every one of us with gifts the measure of faith.

181

(Never seek to be discharged from duty - Matthew 25 and story of the talents).

To present a rusted ax at the judgment seat of Christ will result in us being led to a heap of wood, hay and stubble - cheap materials, instead of the more costly gold, silver and precious stones we would have had if we'd used the implement of divine service when the opportunity was afforded.

3. The ax may have been neglected and become rusty because the owner has rheumatism, arthritis, or some other disease. When one is crippled and bedfast, he can't keep busy at the woodpile. Likewise, disabled and enfeebled believers cannot maintain steady and fruitful service for Christ. Love for the world and its pleasures can produce incapacity that will leave us powerless to help others. An ax left to itself becomes rusty, pitted, useless.

4. The ax has been neglected in the tool shed. A grindstone is essential to a woodsman's equipment. All cutting tools must be submitted to its abrasive surface. If the hone and emery wheel were not rough, they could not achieve their purpose. Trials are the believers' whetstone. They are the designs of a wise, understanding God. They are not unreasonable but are said to be common to man

(1st Co 10: 13). They are not unbearable; they are light afflictions and are brief in duration. They are not a hindrance but are working for us in our behalf to keep the ax of Christian service in working condition. To fail in the time of testing is disastrous. To do so is to come short of divine aim. The crown of life is promised to those who endure. (James 1: 12) We can count it all joy when we are victorious in testing and trials, unto the praise and honor and glory at the appearing of Jesus Christ, if our faith has remained as refiner's gold from refiner's fire.

If we complain and murmur during the process intended four our perfection, we are but refusing the whetstone that God has designed to sharpen our ax. Prayer is another means of keeping the edge on an axe. Because of the faithfulness of two ministers attending a prayer meeting at the beautiful gate a miracle was performed. (Acts 2 1-10) The early Christians petitioned for boldness that resulted in Spiritual earthquake that shook the place where they were gathered together. (Acts 4/23 to 33)

A single cottage prayer meeting caused God to send his angel down when Peter was in prison and rescue him from Herod. (Acts 12: 1-17) We cry because the iron is blunt. We're reaping the harvest of our own neglect - the lack of prayer in our lives. The decreasing number of seekers in our altars and prayer rooms is evidence of our indifference. We find time to stand in back of our auditorium to laugh and talk but we cannot spare a few moments to wait upon the Lord.

The sight of a sinner calling on God for mercy does not stir us anymore. While angels rejoice, some Christians chat and gossip. The reasons some believers tire so easily these days, their strength is spent in using dull implements. Programs are fine, but if they are substituted for divine power, their weakness is apparent.

A little promotion is an advantage, but if it becomes the sole means of our survival, we can expect shipwreck of the shores of spiritual revival. 1 Co 2: 1-5 is our only salvation. When the risen Christ is our whole theme, we can expect to wield an axe that will have the prayer effect on that which it contacts. When we approach our fellow man in humility, fear and trembling, we can have the divine assistance we need. Blunt iron can cut but little wood. A powerless life cannot build the kingdom of God unless you keep the ax sharp. (Eph 2: 21,22)

The Holy Highway

The Lord impressed upon Israel by precept and example - but they went a whoring after strange gods, their neighbor's gods, and finally lost their kingdom and inheritance in Canaan - riches untold for time and eternity. They squandered their valuable inheritance.

Why do people live carelessly, seeking pleasures on the Lord's Day, neglecting worship and praise, withholding their tithes, as though they are independent of the living God?

Proverbs 14: 12: There is a way which seemeth right unto a man, but the end thereof are the ways of death. Solomon, by the wisdom of God, wrote long ago Proverbs 29: 18: Where there is no vision, the people perish: but he that keepeth the law, happy is he.

What is vision and why is it so lacking today? Webster described vision in three ways: natural sight, divine revelation, creation of the imagination. We are fearfully and wonderfully made by our supernatural God and given these ways of sight called vision. But the eyes of earth can always see the desires of their hearts, and seek ways that they may attain. It seems few seek God. Psalms 37:4-5: Delight thyself also in the Lord and he shall give thee the desires of thine heart. Commit thy way unto the Lord, trust also in him and he shall bring it to pass.

1 This is the way of the holy highway that leads to the throne. Many are living in the creation of their imagination instead of believing the Word of God. Jesus says in Luke 12: 15-18: And he said unto them, take heed, and beware of covetousness: for a man's life consists, not in the abundance of the things which he possesses. And he spake a parable unto them, saying, the ground of a certain rich man brought forth plentifully: And he thought within himself, saying, what shall I do, because I have no room where to bestow my fruits? And he said, this will I do: I will pull down my barns, and build greater; and there will I bestow all my fruits and my goods. And I will say to my soul,

Soul, thou hast much goods laid up for many years; take thine ease, eat, drink, and be merry. But God said unto him, thou fool, this night thy soul shall be required of thee: then who's shall those things be, which thou hast provided? So, is he that layeth up treasure for himself, and is not rich toward God? And he said unto his disciples, Therefore I say unto you, take no thought for your life, what ye shall eat; neither for the body, what ye shall put on. The life is more than meat, and the body is more than raiment. Consider the ravens: for they neither sow nor reap; which neither have storehouse nor barn; and God feedeth them: how much more are ye better than the fowls? And which of you with taking thought can add to his stature one cubit? If ye then be not able to do that thing which is least, why take ye thought for the rest? Consider the lilies how they grow: they toil not, they spin not; and yet I say unto you, that Solomon in all his glory was not arrayed like one of these. If then God so clothe the grass, which is to day in the field, and tomorrow is cast into the oven; how much more will he clothe you, "oh ye of little faith"?

The love story of your life may never be published in book form on earth, but in heaven it will be known and shown. On the Holy Highway, there are gates. Isa 62: 10-12: Go through, go through the gates; prepare ye the way of the people; cast up, cast up the highway; gather out the stones; lift up a standard for the people. Behold, the LORD hath proclaimed unto the end of the world, say ye to the daughter of Zion, Behold, thy salvation cometh; behold, his reward is with him, and his work before him. And they shall call them, the holy people, the redeemed of the LORD.

Prophecy: Oh my people, saith the Lord, so important are those truths to thy souls that they must be proclaimed over and over and hammered in by the hammer of God's word until transformed into fiery words of living flame, until hearts are on fire and desires are born to mount this holy highway and go through the gates to the morning of great joy that shall spread itself over the mountain tips as the rising sun of righteousness and grow and glow until every valley is exalted and illuminated and all the earth shall behold the holy banner of God's love in his glorified saints who glorify their Lord. Behold them looking forth as the morning for the coming glory of the morning of God's new day. Paul was on the holy highway doing his best holding the banner high for us.

Philippians 3: 12-14: Not as though I had already attained, either were already perfect: but I follow after, if that I may apprehend that for which also, I am apprehended of Christ Jesus. Brethren, I count not myself to have apprehended: but this one thing I do, forgetting those things which are behind, and reaching forth unto those things which are before, I press toward the mark for the prize of the high calling of God in Christ Jesus.

The pioneers must press to the very gates of the New Jerusalem. The last gates to go through will be those gates of pearl, so typical of our Lords' life and work. A pearl is made in the natural and then the same process is applied in the supernatural. An irritation of some kind invades the oyster's shell home and it cannot be cast out. So patiently the oyster works applying a substance God hath provided, applying it over and over the irritation until a beautiful pearl is formed with its value unknown to the oyster.

Faith that worketh by the love of God covers the irritations of our lives. We can all wear pearls, forgetting ourselves and pressing on to obtain the pearl of great price, which is Jesus.

Philippians 3: 10 That I may know him and power of his resurrection and the fellowship of his sufferings. Oh, that we can lift up a standard for the people. The fig tree hath put forth her green figs, which is Israel. Christ is the vine and we are the branches which bear fruit unto him. But the unripe figs remain

186

on the tree through the winter, but the grapes are gathered in.

Jeremiah 6: 16 Thus saith the Lord: stand ye in the ways and see and ask for the old paths where is the good way and walk therein and ye shall find rest for your souls.

The Most Powerful Power

God's power is not administrated by God on an individual basis or singular basis. What makes it appear like it works that way is because of our faith accidents. We get together and someone releases their faith and someone gets healed and we don't know how we did it.

The reason of that is we've been trying to answer spiritual situations with natural answers, but it doesn't work that way. We've tried to get the spiritual things to act like natural and they won't do it. Those things are spiritual laws. We're dealing with, talking about, and being affected by the most powerful power known - the power of God - the healing power of Almighty God, the saving power of Almighty God, the baptizing power of the Holy Ghost by the Almighty God. That's God's power.

People will say, "Well, you know how powerful the devil is." He's about as powerful compared to God as a whisper in a cyclone. Satan doesn't have no power. Jesus said, "All power is given unto me in heaven and in earth." The Church of Jesus Christ has been letting the devil use our power on us.

We're dealing with the most powerful power in this universe or any other. It is God's power. Therefore, it has to be regulated. It has to have proper demand put on it. It has to be administered properly. Jesus said, talking about this power, that they could jerk a tree up by the roots and slam it into the sea. And the men he was talking to was a long way from the sea. They weren't just standing out there on the seashore. A small amount of this power would do that. A large amount of this power created the whole universe. measuring stick of God's power is measured like this: God's power is measured at the speed of light - the light of this glorious gospel. One writer said the entrance of his word bringeth light. mother said the Bible said God's Chariots traveled from east to west at the speed of lightning.

God said, "Let there be light." At 186,000 miles a second for 24 hours, God created sixteen billion, 240 million miles of universe. You don't know what a billion is, much less 16 billion. If you had a billion dollars while Jesus was on the earth and you spent $1,000 a day until today, you'd still have 240 million left. That's what a billion is. A stack of $1,000 bills 4 inches high is a million. One stack of $1,000 bills 50 stories high is a billion. And in 24 hours' time just because He said, "Light be," there were 16 billion miles of universe slung into action and existence by the same power that made your body, recreated your spirit. And it's the same power that's residing on the inside of you now. God is the one that did it. Now you can understand why that power is regulated.

This Is My Beloved Son

1. It is Jesus Christ I want to find; Pray tell me where he is. It is him alone that can change my mind and give my conscience ease. This is my beloved Son; hear him. This is my beloved Son; hear him.

2. I heard a voice from heaven say, "this is my beloved Son; hear him." If you'll go down in yonder world and search among the sheep, you'll find him there, so I am told, with those he loves to keep.

3. What signal may I find him by from any other man? He wears Salvation on his brow And in His arms, a lamb.

4. I think you, friends, for your advice; I will find him if I can. And if I do, I will rejoice For Christ is a friend of man.

Unsigned, Year Un

Appendix C — The Fleagle Gang

My father told that when he was a teenager two of the Fleagles gang were his friends rented and lived in our house. Dad knew the brothers as Walter and Lee Cook. He often played cards with them and had target practice, shooting into a large oak tree in the front yard. He was in class in high school in Hollister when he learned that his friend Walter Cook had been shot and killed in the railroad station in Branson.

On May 23, 1928, Ralph Fleagle, his brother Jake Fleagle, George J. Abshier, (a.k.a. Bill Messick), and Howard "Heavy" Royston, came in to Lamar, Colorado. They planned to rob the First National Bank. E. A. Lundgren, a one-armed teller at the bank, was waiting on a customer when he saw the men come into the bank and heard one shout, "Hands up!"

Unwisely the bank president, Mr. Parrish, with customers in his bank, using a colt 45 began firing at the nearest bank robber hitting Howard Royston in the face. Mr. Parrish was subsequently shot and killed; his son Jaddo was also killed in the gun fire.

The gang was heavily armed and were prepared for the get away with road maps and also the brothers knew the layout of the county of Prowers in Colorado. They also had license plates for their car from Kansas, Colorado, Oklahoma, and California. They had $10,664 in cash, $12,400 in Liberty Bonds and almost $200,000 in commercial paper they stuffed into pillowcases and took two hostages

189

Edward A. Lundgren and a teller named Everett Kesinger hostages as they made their getaway. They left the bank out to their car by a back door.

The robbers used rifles to disable the sheriff's car at the Sand Creek crossing northeast of Lamar, where, the gang got away. Ralph Fleagle was driving their 1927 blue Buick Master Six car. The gang released the one-armed teller Lundgren.

Back in Kansas by nightfall with Royston who had been wounded the bank president needed medical attention. The gang tricked Dr. Wineinger a local doctor into coming out from his Dighton, Kansas home at night by telling him that a young boy's foot had been crushed by a tractor. When the doctor arrived at the ranch, he discovered the ruse, but treated Royston's wounds. After he finished, the gang shot him in the back of the head with a shotgun, and rolled his body and his Buick into a ravine north of Scott City, Kansas.

Jake Fleagle, alias Walter Cook drove through Branson Tuesday morning at 10 or 11 o'clock. Jake bought a ticket back to Hollister and the two men waited in their Ford sedan until the south bound train arrived. On the train were five police officers, two from Kansas City, two from Los Angeles, one from Colorado Springs and also three postal inspectors. The men who had been following Fleagle for so long had studied the bandits' photograph and physical characteristics so that when he got off the train someplace along the White River Division that morning, they would know him.

Jake Fleagle was clean shaven, but shabbily dressed. He wore an old felt hat, blue overalls, a blue serge coat and a pair of heavy, dark-rimmed glasses. He boarded the train. Through the coach window the FBI spotted Fleagle coming up the Branson platform. The officers moved toward the passenger car entrance. As Jake came into the vestibule and was about to take the first seat facing back through the car, they approached.

"Put 'em up," they said.

Fleagle reached for his gun. One report says he had his finger on the trigger. One of the officers fired into his stomach. Fleaglels' gun hand was grabbed by another officer, and though he was said to have struggled fiercely, he was soon handcuffed and put in leg irons. The lone bullet had emerged from Fleagle's back and was later found embedded in the sill of the coach window.

Occupants of the train scarcely realized what had happened and there was little or no commotion or excitement among them. Before he lapsed into unconsciousness, the wounded man admitted he was Jake Fleagle, but evaded answering other questions. Dr. Guy B. Mitchell and the Whelchel ambulance, were called and the bandit was taken to Dr. Mitchells' office. After an hour, he revived enough that he was taken, under heavy guard, to Springfield Baptist Hospital.

Some people in Branson recognized the wounded man as Walter Cook. The officers, never revealing any prior knowledge of the location of the hideout, drove at once to search the house. Lee Cook was not there. He had apparently been waiting to board the train at the Hollister station. Then the train failed to arrive on time and word spread of a shootout at the Branson station, Lee drove away in the Ford sedan.

In those days, a single finger print was a long shot, but the law got lucky when a transient named William Holden was arrested on suspicion of a train robbery. Holden was later freed after providing a solid alibi, but the sheriff sent his fingerprints to Washington on a hunch. After Fleagle's death, his fingerprints were taken and sent to the FBI, where the right index print was found to be identical with that lone print from the window of the slain Dr. Wineinger's automobile the prints were identified not as belonging to a William Holden, but rather to Jake Fleagle who had served time in the Oklahoma Penitentiary, and matched the print on the car.

Mrs. Cary, who ran the local post office, had identified Cook who actually was Fleagle from seeing him pick up his mail. After the shooting, the inspector came by the store to thank her for her help in confirming Fleagles' identity and whereabouts, many months later, an inspector came back to Ridgedale to the Cary's store, to tell them that

Lee Cook had been caught. The officers did not identify Lee Cook further, nor give any particulars about his career or capture.

It was alleged that some of the money taken in the robbery was buried on our place in Ridgedale. As a small boy, perhaps in my preteens, I took treasure hunters on tours in the woods and hills in back of our house.

And, of course, the whole Fleagle affair was immortalized in verse and song. On January 22, 1931, the White River Leader carried on its front page the words to a Bud Billings Ballad, advertised inside the paper as available on a Victor recording, detailing "The Fate of the Fleagle Gang" song can be heard on YouTube

Appendix D —

A conversation with Uncle Junior that will stay with me for life

After resigning from the Nations Harvest Bible School, I found myself lacking purpose and direction. After prayer, I decided to focus on my extended family. Several cousins on my mother's side lived in Missouri, Texas and Kentucky. I had not seen many of them since we were small children. My brother Rick, and sisters Lavonna and Cleota, and I drove to eastern Kentucky for an impromptu family reunion. We enjoyed the trip very much and created an annual family reunion of our mother's family. Other offspring of my grandparents George and Victoria Youngblood often come from Oklahoma and Texas. We meet the first Saturday in September at the Cedar Valley Community Church in Hollister, Missouri. Ironically, this church started from a revival that our grandfather George, great grandfather Powell, and Uncle Paul preached in Oasis, Missouri in the Cedar Valley school house that was flooded when the Table Rock Dam was built.

I also began visiting my aunts and uncles on my father's side who lived in the southern Missouri area. They included: Aunt Hazel, Buck's wife; Aunt Nadine, Bufford's wife; Clarence and Lora Dean Fisher, my father's sister; and Uncle Junior (EG Dickey), husband of Aunt Lodema (Chattie), dad's sister. I would go a couple times a year, usually on a Saturday and sit and talk. My cousins would tell me how

193

much their parents enjoyed the visits. Later, Rick, Lavonna and Cleota would join me on some of the visits. Over the years that group had all

succumbed to old age. This story is about my final visit to my remaining uncle.

It was raining Saturday, March 8, 2014 when we arrived at the Dickey household. Lavonna, Cleota and Rick entered first and greeted Uncle Junior, who was sitting in a large electrically controlled easy chair. Nearby was a lift that could be used to move him within the house. Gene Autry, dressed as a cavalry sergeant, was on the television. E.G, Dickey (Uncle Junior) he was near 90 years old. As usual he was happy to see us. Cleota and Lavonna both hugged him and Lavonna kissed him on his bald head. As I approached, I heard the familiar "Well I declare, Hobert how are you doing?"

"Doing great," I said, "what about yourself?"

"I'm not doing so good; I keep getting weaker. They finally got that blood loss fixed. Boy they had a time with that. The problem now is they keep drawing blood out of me; I told them you are taking it out faster than I can make it. The good Lord has allowed me to live a long time, this coming June I'll be 91 years old."

"Looks like they are taking good care of you here," I said.

"Man, I'm telling you what, that Renee she looks after me like you can't believe. Renee is an employee of Jerry in his electrical contracting business, and happens to be a nurse, checks on my medicine, gets my breakfast and just makes sure I'm doing good, "I don't know what I would do without her" he said, he was very thankful and wanted to compliment her publicly.

"Uncle Junior, you got to be careful what you are saying, she can hear you, her head will swell up so much that she can't get her hat on," I said.

"Naw," he said, "her head won't swell, she is a good 'en."

The grimace on his face told he was uncomfortable in the position in which he was sitting; using the remote he began to adjust the chair to an upright position. Renee, afraid he would slide out of the chair to the floor, stopped him and readjusted the chair into a position where he was laying back. I watched him relax and give a sigh saying, "Boy that's better."

He said, "I don't know what I would do without my kids, that Kathy and all the grandchildren they are here when I need anything. I know you have children that you are proud of, but I have beyond a doubt, the best son there is on the planet. See that van parked in the front of the house, well I had gotten so weak I couldn't get in the truck anymore and he comes home driving that van the other day. It has a lift so I can get into it and go to the doctor." Big tears began to run down his face. "I just couldn't keep from crying when I saw that van drive in. Now I can go to the doctor when I need to. You know family is so important. You take, that Chatty! I don't believe there is another woman in the world like her. She could meet a total stranger, and within five minutes they would be taking like they had been friends for years."

I grabbed a stool and set down close enough that he could hear me without me talking very loudly. I started by asking questions about his younger years. His demeanor totally changed when I asked a question about his military service.

"What were your responsibilities aboard ship? Were you a gunner? Did you work on the engines?"

"No," he said, "I wasn't assigned as a crew member to a ship, the ship was strictly transport."

"Where did you serve while in the navy?" I asked.

"The Hebrides Islands in the South Pacific."

"Tell me about that," I said, "What exactly did you do?"

As he began to answer my questions it seemed that a fire ignited deep within him. His voice became stronger as he began giving me a detailed account. Those experiences that had happened so long ago once again seemed so real; it was as if they had happened only yesterday.

"We were on a large island," he said. "I don't know its name but we had a repair depot there. Airplanes that needed repaired were brought to us, we repaired them and they went back into the fight. Hobert, have you ever been in a jungle, I mean a jungle in the tropics?"

"No," I said.

He began to tell of how dark it was in the midst of those trees, that sunlight couldn't penetrate to the ground. At night you couldn't see your hands.

"The jeep that dropped us off for guard duty had a small pencil of light. That was the only thing you could see as they came back to pick us up when it was time to change out the guard."

"Were you armed when on guard duty?" I asked.

"Yes," he said, "we had M-1 rifles.

"We didn't see much of the natives on the island. They lived back in the island's interior. You know I did see the oddest thing that I

196

have ever seen in my life. I saw a native woman carrying a baby on her back in a little cradle and that baby was nursing. She was able to get her breast over her shoulder. I never seen anything like it before or since. The natives didn't wear clothes. They wanted to, but they couldn't get them. We would discard our clothes that were worn out and had holes and they would take them and wear them."

"What did you do on the planes?" I asked.

"Engines," Uncle Junior said.

"Can you work on an airplane engine?" I asked.

"No!" He said, "I just changed them out. I would remove the old engine and install a new engine. After I checked that it was operating properly, I moved on to the next plane. There was no quitting at five o clock when there was work to do. The first order of business was to repair the planes and get them back into the fight. I worked continuously until the last one was completed."

"Were there specialists who worked on different aspects of the required repair?" I asked.

"Yes," he said. "There were metallurgists who put on new skin that was shot up or damaged in combat and still others who worked on electronics, etc. There was only one man who was allowed to install, repair, and adjust the engine magnetos. No one touched the magnetos but him."

His voice became strong and animated as he relived those years in the navy. He talked for over an hour. He described a strip of land ten miles long, cleared of trees and used as a runway. Repaired planes were tested on that strip before they were returned to active service.

"It was my job to test the plane's systems after I installed the engine," he said. "After I had installed and tested the new engine, I then taxied the plane to a holding area where other planes were parked, waiting to be picked up and flown back into service. It was my responsibility to certify an air craft was mechanically ready for service.

"Though I never did it, all I would have had to do as I taxied that plane down that strip was pull back on that stick and I could have

197

been flying." The responsibilities of the job, the feeling of power, the roar of the engines and the smell, got into his blood. It gave him strength and a high that he would never forget.

He began the test on the engine in the staging area. After he tied the plane down: at both wings and the tail, he would start the engine and rev it up to 500 rpms and hold it for thirty to forty-five minutes, then 1000 rpms, then 1500, 2000, and then 2200. When it checked out at 2200 rpms for an hour, he marked it as ok and ready for service.

"Those days and experiences are just as real as if it was yesterday. I wouldn't give fifteen cents to do it again but wouldn't take a million dollars for the experience," he said.

He recalled some kind of a memorial statue had been placed on the island by the Japanese. Every so often a small single engine Japanese plane would fly over, too high for anti-aircraft guns to reach, fly around for a while and leave. He said, "The planes we had were bombers, much too heavy and slow to engage that little plane."

"One day" he said, "we modified one of our bombers, stripped out all guns but one, and removed the bomb racks. The amount of fuel was limited to keep the plane as light as possible. The little Japanese plane in its normal pattern showed up as usual. The specially designed bomber was launched and attacked the Japanese plane from above and behind; that little plane didn't return to base."

Hogs, cattle and horses were wild on the island and when time permitted, they would hunt. There were those on the islands, who for a fee, would take you hunting. It was illegal to hunt cattle unless they were destroying property. Property damage seemed to be a common occurrence; they ate a lot of steak. Wild hogs were a nuisance and fresh pork was a regular item of their diet.

He wasn't sure where he was when President Truman dropped the bomb. After the war was over, he returned to the States at San Francisco. Every plane, bus and train were full, with no way to get home. A group of sailors from the Midwest found a private individual who had a bus. When he was contacted, he had just returned from a trip and had had no sleep. They begged him to take them home. He agreed if they would drive while he got some sleep. Uncle Junior was the main bus driver for a full day and most of the night. He was dropped off at the front door of his home.

We had talked nonstop for most of an hour. Realizing he must be getting tired; I made a date to see him at a pig roast in June. (This was an annual birthday bash for Uncle Jr.)

He said, "Yes, Jerry has promised me if I felt like it there would be another pig roast." He said it was something that he looked forward to. He felt it was good for the neighborhood. People could get together and reconnect. Sometimes we just get too busy and neglect the important things in life. Yes, he would plan on the pig roast in June. "Most of my family are gone, just me and Eugene is left, and I'll be 91 years old my next birthday in June." We all did meet at the pig roast later in June; Uncle Junior died soon after.

As I was leaving Jerry and Renee, using the chair, helped him stand up for a moment. His weakness had returned, his voice was strained as he was attempting to help as much as he could.

The End

Made in United States
Troutdale, OR
07/28/2024

21598314R00116